U.S. Industrial
Competitiveness

U.S. Industrial Competitiveness

The Case of the Textile and Apparel Industries

Fariborz Ghadar
George Washington University

William H. Davidson
University of Southern California

Charles S. Feigenoff
International Management Center

Lexington Books
D.C. Heath and Company/Lexington, Massachusetts/Toronto

Library of Congress Cataloging-in-Publication Data

Ghadar, Fariborz.
  U.S. industrial competitiveness.

  Includes index.
  1. Textile industry—United States. 2. Clothing
trade—United States. 3. Competition, International.
I. Davidson, William Harley, 1951–   . II. Feigenoff,
Charles Samuel. III. Title. IV. Title: US industrial
competitiveness. V. Title: United States industrial
competitiveness.
HD9855.G47 1987   338.4′7677′00973   86-46341
ISBN 0-669-15689-2 (alk. paper)

Published simultaneously in Canada
Printed in the United States of America
Casebound International Standard Book Number: 0-669-15689-2
Library of Congress Catalog Card Number: 86-46341

The paper used in this publication meets the minimum requirements of American
National Standard for Information Sciences—Permanence of Paper for Printed Library
Materials, ANSI Z39.48-1984. ∞™

87 88 89 90 8 7 6 5 4 3 2 1

Contents

Tables and Figures

Preface

T he ability of the United States to compete in the world economy, especially in the manufacturing sector, has declined sharply in the last fifteen years. The editors of the recently completed report entitled *U.S. Competitiveness in the World Economy* note the shift "from decades of trade surpluses to substantial deficits, eroding market share in almost all sectors, and declining profitability since the late 1960s." They also point out that real after-tax earnings of American workers have declined since their peak in 1972. This challenge to the U.S. economy is not entirely a matter of private-sector shortcomings. Public policies that encourage consumer borrowing and penalize savings, for instance, have also contributed to the decline. Seen in the longer view, however, the erosion of competitiveness is relative, not absolute. Foreign competitors have simply outpaced U.S. industry as a result of superior private- and public-sector efforts and achievements. This competition has not come from our traditional competitors. We have done as well as if not better than our European counterparts on international markets in recent years. Our major competitors have been Japan and, to an increasing extent, a second tier of powerful exporters, led by Taiwan, South Korea, Singapore, and Hong Kong.

The purpose of this book is to examine the global and domestic forces that have affected the performance of the U.S. manufacturing sector. These forces are complex in nature, and many were unimagined twenty years ago. We will examine the corporate and governmental responses to these developments and will discuss recommendations that have been made to increase the competitiveness of U.S. industry. Our intent is not prescriptive. Rather, the book is an account, based on statistical evidence and firsthand consultation, of the evolution of the present crisis in competitiveness and a description of the solutions that have been advanced to address it.

The U.S. textile and apparel industries have been chosen to illustrate this account because they play a significant and extraordinarily complex role in this country's economy. The well-being of several industrial and agricultural sectors depends on them. Apparel sales are the most important merchandise category for department stores, mass merchandisers, and specialty stores. On the other end of the production chain, the agricultural sector provides the cotton and wool necessary for the manufacture of natural fibers. Petrochemicals provide the basic feedstock for most manmade fibers (excluding cellulosics such as rayon, acetate, and triacetate) and for dyeing and fabric treatments. The textile machinery and equipment industry, a subsector of machinery manufacture, is also dependent on the textile industry. Standard & Poor's estimated that in 1983, nine hundred thousand jobs among suppliers were required to support the industry.

These two industries also represent the largest manufacturing sector in the U.S. economy. The textile milling and apparel manufacturing industries employ approximately 1.9 million people, or 10 percent of the American manufacturing work force. Textile mills are located in forty-eight states, and the industry is one of the primary employers in many nonurban communities. Apparel firms are found in every state and are particularly important in the metropolitan areas of the Middle Atlantic states and in California. The textile apparel industry is also the largest industrial employer of women and minority workers. In 1984, for example, minorities constituted 27 percent of the apparel manufacturing work force, while women made up 81 percent, the highest percentage of any manufacturing industry. In 1984, better than one out of every six women employed in the United States manufacturing sector worked in textiles or apparel.

Of course, the textile and apparel industries, considered both as closely related industries and as distinct segments of the manufacturing sector, have unique characteristics and face unique problems. But because the textile and apparel industries have for many years wrestled with the problem of increasing competition in the international marketplace, a problem that other U.S. industries have only begun to face in the last decade, they can be considered vanguard industries. Their special characteristics are illuminating, even though there is much legitimate disagreement among those involved in the textile and apparel industries about the effectiveness of the corporate and governmental approaches that have been relied on to improve competitiveness and about those strategies which are to be implemented in the future. The differences between these two and other U.S. industries highlight the issues that the U.S. manufacturing sector as a whole must face as it seeks to restore its competitiveness on the world markets.

Acknowledgments

This book grew out of a study undertaken on behalf of the National Chamber Foundation. As such, it has benefited from the guidance and assistance of the Chamber Foundation staff and the men and women from the textile, apparel, and retailing industries who sat on our advisory board. Our work on this book entailed a process of repeated reorganization and refinement, and our understanding of the issues was broadened by the diverse perspectives that the members of this panel—leaders of major U.S. corporations, prominent economists, and experts from the public and private sector in trade and technology— brought to our discussions of U.S. competitiveness.

There are, however, no easy answers to this problem, and we accept full responsibility for whatever oversights we have committed in our evaluation of the textile and apparel industries and in our application of the lessons learned in these two industries to the manufacturing sector as a whole. We wish to state that the opinions expressed in this book are our own and do not necessarily reflect those of the Chamber Foundation or members of the advisory board.

1
An Overview

The textile and apparel industries have been chosen to illustrate this study of U.S. industrial competitiveness because they play a significant and extraordinarily complex role in the U.S. economy. Together, they are the largest employer in the manufacturing sector, with approximately 1.9 million workers, or 10 percent of the American manufacturing labor force. In addition, the well-being of several other industrial and agricultural sectors depends on them. Furthermore, because the textile and apparel industries have for many years wrestled with the problem of increasing international competition, a problem that other U.S. industries have begun to face only in the last decade, they can be considered vanguard industries.

There is much legitimate disagreement among those involved in the textile and apparel industries about the effectiveness of corporate and governmental policies that have been relied on to improve competitiveness to date. Even greater debate attends discussion of possible future policy directions. These factors highlight the issues that the U.S. manufacturing sector as a whole must face as it seeks to restore its competitiveness on the world markets. This book sheds light on the realities of global competition and the way two industries coped with this phenomenon.

The Question of Adjustment

The problem of adjustment can basically be considered twofold. On the one hand, it is a domestic problem affecting a particular industry within a national economy. Adjustment involves restoring the productivity of an industry so that it remains competitive in the overall industrial scheme of the economy. Adjustment in this context often occurs through the rationalization of existing firms and facilities in order to establish a few large, efficient producers and a number of specialized vendors. Rationalization can be guided either by market forces or by public policy. Although publicly guided rationalization has been common in other countries' textile industries (notably those of Japan, France, and the United Kingdom), U.S. traditions emphasize a more market-driven process. Market realities force firms to take appropriate steps to close or automate facilities, add or drop product lines, acquire or be acquired by other firms, and otherwise find means of improving competitiveness or redeploying resources to other industries. Increased competitiveness can result from a number of private corporate initiatives, such as a commitment to research and development, the implementation of automated equipment and more efficient procedures, and a reevaluation of marketing strategies.

Adjustment also has an international dimension, reflected in the relationship of the national economy to that of its trading partners. Adjustment in this sense is achieved primarily through changes in exchange rates and through the regulation of trade. The national and international adjustment processes are interrelated. Industrial sectors that increase productivity faster than the overall national economy should become more competitive in the international economy. However, exchange rate movements can dramatically affect the competitiveness and trade performance of national economies and individual industries within an economy. An overvalued dollar can cause intrinsically healthy sectors to register losses and can even lead to their elimination. During these periods, government policy may turn to trade regulation to give these industries time to cope with change in the international economy.

Change in the International Marketplace

One essential impetus for adjustment in U.S. industry during the last thirty years has been the emergence of a new set of export-oriented countries in the world economy. In the textile industries, these newly industrialized countries (NICs) play a major role. The most obvious advantage the NICs enjoy is their low labor costs. Furthermore, they target export-oriented industries for development and enact measures designed to protect their home market from overseas competition while these industries are growing. These factors have allowed the NICs to become competitive with the United States and other countries belonging to the Organization for Economic Cooperation and Development (OECD) across an increasingly wide spectrum of industries.

These same factors can be clearly seen in the case of the textile and apparel industries. Several Third World countries with a relative abundance of labor have developed large, rapidly growing textile and apparel industries. In 1985, according to U.S. Department of Commerce reports, the four leading exporters of textiles and apparel to the United States were Taiwan, Korea, Hong Kong, and China. Together they accounted for 45.2 percent of all the textile and apparel imports into the United States. The distorted value of the dollar aggravated this situation by causing a shift in their trade from other OECD nations to the United States. At the same time, U.S. manufacturers, in textiles and other industries, have only limited access to the growing domestic markets of these countries because of their restrictive trade policies.

Textiles and apparel were among the earliest industries affected by international competition owing to the nature of the industries themselves. The textile and apparel industries have traditionally been the means by which less developed countries begin their pursuit of industrialization. The raw materials of textile and apparel manufacture are relatively common, and both textile and apparel require less capital than most other manufactures. The production of textiles and apparel makes these basic industries extremely attractive, first as a source of import substitution and eventually as a primary source of export earnings with which to further economic and social development. Typically, a developing country enters developed foreign markets with low-value-added exports, but as its domestic industry grows and evolves, product lines are broadened to include man-made and synthetic fibers. The lower-value-added products in all fiber types are eventually cast off, and, in turn, become the basic exports for lower-wage-base countries.

Textiles and Apparel in the 1970s

During the 1970s, the textile industry and, to a lesser extent, the apparel industry made significant strides in achieving the adjustment necessary to counter the increasing international competitiveness of the NICs. Textile productivity grew at a much faster rate than the economy as a whole. This was achieved by committing substantial outlays for new plants and equipment designed to increase manufacturing efficiency and versatility. In addition to reducing production costs and improving the quality of fabrics, the newer technology also permitted the production of more complicated products with shorter start-up times. One of the primary goals of these modernization efforts was to increase specialization in segments where the U.S. industry enjoys a leadership position and has strong market acceptance. Restoring the competitiveness of the apparel industry has been more difficult because of the structure of the industry and the labor-intensive nature of the product. Traditionally, apparel was a family industry comprised of thousands of small companies averaging less than a hundred employees and producing an extremely narrow product line. It has also been an industry where production changes have come very slowly. However, the apparel industry began to experience a major restructuring in the 1970s, with the result that its productivity grew slightly faster than that of the industrial sector as a whole. The larger firms' share of total output increased; the capital and knowledge intensity of the industry grew; and the product lines produced by many apparel firms were widened and upgraded. Textile and apparel companies have continued their efforts to increase productivity even through the more trying conditions of the 1980s.

The textile and apparel industries, in general, performed strongly during the 1970s. Their level of growth was on a par with, and in some sectors exceeded, that of the economy as a whole. They addressed the issue of adjustment more effectively and at a far more acceptable social cost than their OECD counterparts. There was a steady rise in the dollar value of textile shipments after the low point in the 1975 recession. Shipments grew by 24 percent during the decade (adjusted for inflation), while exports doubled. Although total employment in textiles has declined by 44 percent in the past twenty-five years, this decline has been fairly gradual until recent years. Faced with similar pressure for adjustment, the textile and apparel industries in major OECD countries fared far worse. The end result of the restructuring process in Great Britain, France, West Germany, and Japan is that the textile and apparel industries have declined by at least 50 percent in employment during the past twenty years, and their importance in the overall economic performance of these countries has diminished. Only Italy has maintained textile and apparel industries that are both vital and growing. Despite this major restructuring of the OECD textile and manufacturing sector, increases in productivity lagged behind those achieved by the U.S. industry.

The stability and moderation imposed by the Multifiber Arrangement (MFA) were significant factors in the ability of the textile and apparel industries to sustain their adjustment efforts during the 1970s. In providing a forum for large-scale negotiations among parties of sharply conflicting interests, these conditions gave the textile industry time to revitalize itself. Some critics maintain that the costs of the adjustment were borne by the U.S. consumer and that U.S. companies could have pursued a more extensive and vigorous policy of restructuring. Nonetheless, during the 1970s, a period when the prices of textile and apparel products increased slower than overall U.S. inflation, the textile and apparel industries made important efforts to improve their international competitiveness by increasing their productivity, and, on the whole, these efforts were successful.

Textiles and Apparel in the 1980s

The surge of imports during the 1980s, however, undermined much of the progress achieved in the previous decade. It also created the sense of crisis that infuses the industry today. Since 1981, textile imports have grown rapidly. Imports have risen even more dramatically in apparel. It is estimated that for every dollar's worth of apparel exported in the past three years, nearly $19 worth was imported; also, that one out of every three garments sold in the United States in the same period was manufactured overseas. Higher ratios are prevalent for items like sweaters and women's cotton slacks and shorts. Most of these imports come from the NICs.

The rise in the dollar closely correlates with this exponential growth in imports of textiles and apparel. Although the dollar began its rise in value in 1981, there was a lag time of approximately eighteen months to two years before the apparel and textile markets reflected this growth. Between 1982 and 1983, for instance, textile imports rose by 14.9 percent and apparel imports rose by 17.4 percent. In the next year, however, textile imports rose by 47.2 percent, while apparel imports rose by 44.7 percent. The effects of the inordinately strong dollar on U.S. exports of textiles and apparel were more immediate. In 1982, although they had increased gradually since 1971, exports of apparel abruptly dropped by 25 percent. A similar phenomenon was observable in textile exports, which having risen since 1976, fell by 24 percent in 1981. Another factor contributing to the crisis in textiles and apparel is that the bilateral agreements worked out under the MFA do not subject the majority of product categories to specific import restraints. In addition, many recent agreements that include restrictions on specific products do not control aggregate import ceilings. Furthermore, many critics maintain that U.S. monitoring agencies have not enforced the MFA aggressively. Other observers argue that industry efforts to achieve adjustment have not been as well conceived or as far-reaching as they might have been. The underlying issue, then, is how rapidly a sector must adjust.

These factors—the rise in the value of the dollar and loopholes in existing arrangements—as well as the need, in some sectors of the textile and apparel industries, to improve productivity, have contributed to the present crisis in these industries. Performance in the textile industry slowed considerably in the third and fourth quarters of 1984 and declined sharply through the first half of 1985. Employment in textiles is also down sharply. In June 1985, the U.S. Bureau of Labor Statistics reported that total employment had declined by 7 percent since June 1984. The apparel industry has been hit even harder.

The effect of these losses is long-term. Because the profit margin in textiles and apparel is low, abrupt increases in the value of the dollar, and even small changes therein, can cause firms that would otherwise have remained vigorous to fail. And those that survive will take several years to reestablish lost markets, if these markets can be reestablished at all. At the same time, measures taken to reverse this process and to provide the textile and apparel industries with the environment necessary to continue to adjust must be considered carefully because they affect other sectors of the U.S. economy. This is particularly true in regard to the retailing sector, as apparel sales constitute the most important merchandise category for department stores, mass merchandisers, and specialty stores. Compounding this problem for retailers is an excess of selling space and a corresponding drop in profitability per square foot; retailers will, accordingly, be particularly sensitive to any changes in trade policy which will raise their costs.

One way of achieving results from the significant adjustment efforts taken by the textile and apparel industries is through exchange-rate realignment in the international economy. The inordinate strength of the U.S. dollar has been a serious impediment to the continued viability of the textile and apparel industries and to that of other sectors of the economy as well. Although the value of the dollar has dropped significantly in the past year, it has done so primarily against other developed countries. As a result, U.S. producers of textiles and apparel have substantially restored competitiveness in relation to our OECD trading partners. However, there has been no significant movement against the currencies of the four major textile exporters to the United States. The value of the dollar stayed constant or increased in 1986, compared to the currencies of China, Taiwan, Hong Kong, and South Korea, which together supply almost half of U.S. imports in textiles and apparel. Aggravating this situation is the persistence, in these nations and in Hong Kong, of trade policies geared to limiting imports and promoting exports. It is unlikely that appropriate foreign exchange adjustments in this area will occur in the near future. The alternative is to effect international adjustment through U.S. trade policy. This would require developing more stringent trade restrictions and more consistent enforcement.

One way to determine whether adjustment in the international environment should be pursued, either through the exchange rate or through trade policy, is to examine the performance of the industry itself within the national economy. If the industry continues to adjust and to improve performance at rates exceeding the average for the manufacturing sector as a whole—as the textile and apparel industries have done, even through the difficult times of the 1980s—efforts should be taken to prevent sudden surges in imports resulting from inappropriate currency values or trade policies of other nations. Such steps will permit timely adjustment without massive dislocations. The alternative is to lose a viable industry.

Lessons to Be Learned

The lessons to be learned from the experience of the U.S. textile and apparel industries are several. The most important one is that successful adjustment requires a cooperative effort on the part of private industry and government policymakers. Another lesson, from the industry point of view, is the importance of investment in modernization. Compared to the rest of the manufacturing sector, the textile and apparel industries have invested a high share of their resources in efforts to introduce new technology. These efforts have been responsible for significant increases in the rate of productivity and for these industries' strong showing when compared to the textile and apparel industries of most of our OECD counterparts. A third lesson to be learned from the experience of these industries is that changes in the market require more attention to the market. Declining competitiveness has often been a result of unswerving emphasis on production. In their efforts to remain competitive, the textile and apparel industries have begun to place greater importance on marketing. Indeed, it is marketing considerations that have been the guiding force behind the deployment of new technology. New, flexible manufacturing systems permit greater responsiveness and speed in developing and delivering new, customized products to consumers.

There are also lessons to be learned from the U.S. experience with the MFA. During the 1970s, the MFA provided for a reasonable rate of growth in imports, thereby creating a climate that allowed the textile and apparel industries to adjust to the fundamental changes in world markets in a reasonably controlled fashion. During this period, textile and apparel prices rose at a rate substantially lower than the rate of inflation. However, the MFA and U.S. trade-policy administration have failed to control the industrial environment effectively in the 1980s, in the face of much more rapidly changing market conditions and exchange rates. The conclusions to be drawn from this are threefold. First, the mechanisms in place under agreements like the MFA can no longer be predicated on the relatively stable worldwide financial conditions that existed in the 1960s and early 1970s. Government must be able to respond to the new realities of foreign exchange markets, in which currency values may not respond to trade performance or where trade results may be an accommodation to capital movements. Second, the U.S. response to trade policies that promote exports and restrict imports must be reevaluated. The third and possibly more fundamental conclusion is that even if these first two changes were instituted, not all industries would be able to benefit from them or from arrangements like the MFA. The textile industry performed relatively strongly under the MFA; a low-wage, high-value-added industry like apparel performed less well.

The new relationships that have emerged in the textile and apparel industries—although they are still in their formative stage—have several important implications for U.S. industry as a whole. First, even sectors that are generally agreed to be as beleaguered as textiles and apparel can still make significant structural adjustment. Although the competitiveness of the U.S. manufacturing sector has declined in the past fifteen to twenty years, it has not reached the point where it cannot recoup these losses. Second, significant structural adjustment has been accomplished without extensive direct intervention by the government. There has been much discussion about the need to emulate the Japanese system or to adjust our national priorities so that they more closely resemble those of the NICs. The experience of the textile and apparel industries demonstrates that such direct intervention is unnecessary. As we have seen in the case of our OECD trade partners, direct public intervention or publicly led rationalization may in fact be counterproductive. There exist within our own economic system both the means and will to achieve industrial adjustment and to restore our industrial competitiveness. Yet no industry can remain unaffected by an 80 percent increase in the value of the dollar, a rise that is especially damaging to industries with low profit margins, no matter how well they have been adjusting under more normal circumstances. In such cases, some government intervention is warranted to maintain an even playing field and an environment in which healthy, long-term adjustment can occur.

2
The Decline of U.S. Industrial Competitiveness

The decline in U.S. competitiveness is clearly evident in the performance of the manufacturing sector. The trade balance for manufacturing goods shrank from strong surpluses in the early 1960s to the alarming deficits we face at the present time. The trade deficit in 1985 reached a record $148.5 billion, and the 1986 deficit was even higher. The deficits experienced in these two years exceeded the cumulative total of all previous U.S. trade deficits. U.S. Department of Commerce figures reveal that during this time, U.S. firms experienced declining profitability while losing market share. Market share decreased from 26 to 18 percent between 1960 and 1980, and indicators compiled by Allen Sinai and Allen Lin for Data Resources show that the balance sheet for U.S. firms was at an all-time low in 1982, although the situation has improved somewhat since then. In addition, Department of Commerce statistics reveal that the rate of return adjusted for inflation of U.S. corporations has declined steadily since the mid-1960s. Furthermore, because net investment in plant and equipment has fallen from 4 percent of GNP between 1966 and 1970 to 2 percent in 1982, growth in manufacturing productivity has lagged behind that of major competitors like Japan.

During the 1983–85 period, as the economy emerged from recession, there was a substantial improvement in the condition of the manufacturing sector, though indicators show that the rate of improvement has slowed significantly. Overall, industrial production rebounded by 23 percent between 1982 and 1984; by mid-1984, manufacturing output was 9 percent above its previous peak, while unemployment dropped to 7.5 percent. Labor productivity in the manufacturing sector rose from between 3 and 4 percent annually, and corporate profits and investment both registered an upswing. However, despite improvement in domestic performance, the deterioration of U.S. international competitiveness has accelerated markedly during the 1980s. Over the past four years, the U.S. share of world manufactures exports has fallen by more than 25 percent in volume terms. Since 1970, the import share of the U.S. domestic market has more than doubled, from 8 percent to a little under 19 percent in 1984.

The decline in U.S. competitiveness has been attributed to a variety of sources. Primary among these has been the strength of the dollar. During the 1970s, when the U.S. dollar weakened against other currencies, imports were limited primarily to those regions whose cost functions were much lower than those of the United States. From 1979 to the present, however, as the dollar strengthened, exports were reduced and imports increased significantly. Since the summer of 1980, the U.S. dollar has risen in value by an unprecedented 80 percent or more against major worldwide currencies. While this economic trend has been attractive to Americans who travel abroad or who choose to purchase imported goods, it has had a decidedly negative effect on the U.S. manufacturing sector. The strong dollar has resulted in a decrease of several percentage points in U.S. economic growth; has helped to produce the record trade deficit; and, according to some sources, has eliminated more than 2 million manufacturing jobs. While the dollar has recently declined in relation to the currencies of the European Economic Community (EEC) and Japan, it has not declined in relation to many NICs.

In their report on the President's Commission on Industrial Competitiveness, Rimmer de Vries, senior vice president of Morgan Guaranty Trust Company, and Derek Hargreaves, vice president of the bank, said that the exclusive emphasis on the overvalued dollar is misleading. In their estimation, "a little more than a third of the overall downturn in the U.S. trade or current account position can be ascribed to dollar strength. Roughly another third results from laggard economic performance in most other industrial countries, while the remainder stems from the financial problems of Latin America." They point to such problems as the plunge in U.S. exports to debt-ridden Latin American countries after 1982 and the deterioration of the U.S. trade balance with its OECD partners.

De Vries and Hargreaves also acknowledge one of the most dramatic events in the international marketplace in the last twenty-five years: the emergence of the newly industrialized countries in East Asia. These countries currently enjoy a greater trade surplus with the United States than does the EEC. NICs have industrialized quite rapidly, though their growth was not significant until the early 1960s. World Bank tables show that the annual growth rate in manufacturing of South Korea between 1960 and 1970 was a spectacular 17.6 percent, a rate that continued almost unabated through the decade of the seventies. Taiwan, Hong Kong, Singapore, and Thailand all recorded close to double-digit growth or better during this period, and Indonesia and Malaysia attained double-digit growth in the seventies. Manufactures in Korea and Taiwan, which constituted less than 20 percent of exports in 1960, increased to almost 90 percent in 1980. Concurrent with this growth in the manufacturing sector has been a swing toward segments that require more advanced technology. The NICs have made strong gains in recent years in consumer electronics, telecommunications, watches, and electric machinery.

Several reasons are given for the emergence of the NICs in the world economy. The most obvious reason is their low labor costs. Indonesian pay rates, for instance, average forty cents an hour. The NICs are also high-investment countries. They invest a greater share of GNP than do the developed countries, and they have constructed financial policies that encourage the mobility of capital and labor. Furthermore, they target export-oriented industries for development. They give these industries freer access to imports of raw materials, intermediate goods, and machinery, and they provide financial incentives for exporting, such as tax relief, cheaper finance, or direct-cash subsidies. Finally, they enact measures designed to protect their home market from overseas competition while these industries are growing. These factors have allowed the NICs to become competitive with the United States across an increasingly wide spectrum of industries.

Another cause is offered for the decline of U.S. competitiveness by William Abernathy and Robert Hayes in the *Harvard Business Review*, by Robert Reich in his *Atlantic* exposé, and by Reich and Ira Magaziner in their book, *Minding America's Business*. It is that complacent management has allowed competitors, particularly Japanese competitors, to pull ahead in cost or quality or both. Excessive concern with analysis and planning, internal structure, and short-term results has pushed the interest in innovative manufacturing processes and high-quality products into the background. Although this charge is difficult to evaluate, it appears that poor management has hurt U.S. performance in such areas as automobiles and steel.

Reich and Magaziner, among other commentators, stress the lack of a coherent industrial policy and the need for increased government cooperation with business. In their view, such decision making as occurs is carried out on an ad hoc basis and tends to create adversarial relationships among the parties involved. Bruce R. Scott, however, argues that though implicit, American policy is not incoherent but rather emphasizes the promotion of growth through domestic demand (government spending and personal consumption), in contrast to other countries, which aim to promote growth through external demand (exports and the investments necessary to support them). In his view, the United States has taken its overall competitiveness for granted and has placed higher priority on "distributing the pie than in baking more or better pie." He advocated the adoption of what he calls "growth/productivity-oriented strategies."

No matter what their point of view, most commentators are agreed that the causes, both short- and long-term, of the decline in U.S. competitiveness on international markets are complex and interrelated, and that they should not be treated as if they were separate and unrelated phenomena. Measures designed to treat one cause alone, as de Vries and Hargreaves take pains to demonstrate, will not effectively improve conditions, and indeed will often produce problems of their own.

The Case of the Textile and Apparel Industries

Although the telltale signs of declining competitiveness began to appear in the overall manufacturing sector during the late 1960s and early 1970s, the textile and apparel industries were among the first to face significant international competition and to experience weakened performance on international markets. In this respect, their example is instructive for the rest of the manufacturing sector.

An Overview of the Textile and Apparel Industries

There are approximately six thousand textile mills in the United States, concentrated in such southern states as North Carolina, South Carolina, and Georgia. The major U.S. fabric-producing firms are Burlington Industries, J.P.Stevens, Milliken, West Point-Pepperell, Collins and Aikman, and Springs Mills. Following World War II, the U.S. textile labor force was composed primarily of white, middle-aged males. Now, however, U.S. textile workers are increasingly likely to be young, nonwhite, and female. To some extent, changes in the age and sex composition of the textile labor force have reflected general changes in the overall working population, but they also reflect changes within the industry itself. One nondemographic factor that has influenced the U.S. textile labor force is industrial growth in southeastern states. This expanding industrialization multiplied employment options and contributed to the concentration of women and minorities in the industry, as more mobile or skilled workers left. Approximately 51 percent of the textile work force are women, and 22 percent are minorities.

In 1984, the average hourly earnings of production workers was $6.46, an increase of 22 percent over levels in 1980. Salary and wages plus fringe benefits are significant in textiles, representing only a moderately lower proportion of costs than do raw materials. In fiscal 1983,

Burlington Industries, Fieldcrest Mills, J.P. Stevens, and West Point-Pepperell reported ratios of total labor costs to sales averaging around 30 percent.

The apparel industry in the United States is more fragmented than the textile industry and considerably more volatile. Apparel is considered an unskilled or semiskilled industry, and an entrepreneur who wants to break in does not need extensive capitalization. Most companies have preferred to rely on innate fashion sense rather than professional marketing expertise. Many firms are thinly capitalized, labor-intensive, and focused on the domestic market. All these factors contribute to the rapidly changing nature of the industry and to the high rate of bankruptcy among competitors. According to Dun & Bradstreet, 250 apparel establishments failed in 1983 alone.

Department of Commerce figures indicate that as of 1984 there was a total of twenty-one thousand plants and fifteen thousand producers in the apparel industry, 51 percent of which employed fewer than 20 employees. The average number of employees per establishment was 56. By contrast, in the textile industry, more than two-thirds of the work force was employed in plants with at least 250 employees. Of the apparel manufacturers, 59 percent are concentrated in four states: New York, California, Pennsylvania, and New Jersey. In general, high-fashion and tailored clothing producers are located in the metropolitan areas of the Middle Atlantic states (New York, New Jersey, and Pennsylvania) and in California. Plants producing such products as jean-cut casual slacks, which can be produced in large-volume production runs, are generally located in the southern and southwestern states. There has been a fair amount of concentration in recent years as smaller, marginal firms have been driven from the market. As of 1983, thirty apparel companies with $200 million or more in sales accounted for about 40 percent of the output of apparel. The largest apparel-producing firms in the United States are Levi Strauss, Blue Bell, V.F. Corp., Hartmarx Corp., and Cluett, Peabody and Co.

The apparel industry is the seventh largest U.S. industrial employer, with an average of 1.2 million workers in 1984. The number of production workers in apparels was 1.0 million. Employment in apparels has remained fairly steady, declining by only 6 percent in the last twenty-five years. This figure is a reflection of the labor-intensive nature of production; production workers account for 85 percent of the total work force, compared to 69 percent in all manufacturing. Women and minorities are also heavily represented. According to Department of Commerce statistics, approximately 81 percent of the apparel work force are women and 27 percent are minorities. In 1984, the average hourly earnings of production workers was $5.53. This represents an increase of 18 percent over levels in 1980, but is is still significantly lower than the $9.17 an hour earned by workers in all manufacturing industries.

The Textile and Apparel Industries in the Context of the U.S. Manufacturing Sector

Compared to other industries, the textile and apparel industries are relatively labor intensive, although many of the jobs do not require highly skilled operators. Ten percent of the U.S. manufacturing work force is employed by the textile and apparel industries. Further, these two industries together constitute the largest industrial employer of women and minority workers. In 1984, better than one out of every six women employed in the United States worked in the textile and apparel industries. However, growth in employment lagged considerably behind figures from the industrial sector as a whole. Department of Commerce figures for 1984 show that employment in the U.S. manufacturing sector rose by 4 percent overall. Employment in textiles shrank by 2 percent while employment in apparel increased by 1 percent. Unemployment in the apparel industry averaged 10.8 percent in 1983, and in the textile industry, it ran 8.6 percent, compared to a manufacturing average of 7.5 percent.

The importance of the textile and apparel industries can be measured by other standards as well. Together they generate a gross national product in excess of $48 billion, compared with $51 billion for the auto industry, $43.1 billion for primary metals, and $31.6 billion for petroleum refining in 1984. However, they have not grown as fast as other industries have. According to the Bureau of the Census, the average annual rate of increase of textile-mill output (measured in constant dollars) between 1970 and 1982 was less than 1.5 percent. This is about half the rate for manufacturing as a whole. Total value of textile and apparel industry shipments of $115 billion in 1984 was up from $107 billion in 1983. Figures for 1985 showed a significantly slower growth rate as inventories were reduced, while preliminary indications for 1986 suggest zero growth as total value for combined shipments have remained about the same as 1985.

In 1982, production in the textile industry reached 124.5 percent over production in 1967. This is well below the 138.8 percent level achieved in all manufacturing sectors. Performance in certain areas, however, has been especially strong. Knit goods and carpeting all registered 1982 shipment levels above 170 percent of the 1967 base. However, Department of Labor estimates show that textile productivity growth has been relatively high in the past two decades. From 1970 to 1982, the average annual rate of growth was 3.5 percent. This is consid-

erably stronger than the 2.3 percent growth in productivity in all manufacturing. The overall picture is that of an industry responding to
growth opportunities in certain segments and increasing productivity to
improve profits and competitiveness. Despite these efforts, however,
imports have continued to capture a growing share of the U.S. market,
causing relatively slow growth in shipments by domestic producers.

The major cause for slow growth in industry output has been competition from imports. Imports of textiles and apparel have run higher
than imports in the manufacturing sector as a whole. Department of
Commerce figures show that in 1984, imports of textiles increased by
39 percent over the previous year and imports of apparel increased by 41
percent, while imports of all manufactured goods rose by 33 percent.
Textiles and apparel amounted to 5.5 percent of total imports.

Another important characteristic of the textile and apparel industries is that they show a relatively modest return on sales, which makes
them vulnerable to rapid shifts in the economy. Low profit margins in
apparel production result from the intense competition from both domestic and foreign sources and the relatively small scale of operations.
The textile industry also exhibits relatively low returns. In 1980, a com-
paratively stable year, the profit per dollar of sales in the manufacturing
sector was 4.9 percent, compared to a profit per dollar of sales in textiles
of 2.2 percent. For all manufacturing industries, the profit on total assets
was 7.1 percent, and the profit on stockholders' equity was 13.4 percent.
In the textile industry, the profit on assets was 4.4 percent, while the
profit on stockholders' equity was 8.5 percent.

In general, the textile and apparel industries are characterized by
high reinvestment, high productivity, and low profit margins.

The Emergence of the NICs

The emergence of the NICs has played a major role in the increasing
level of competition in the U.S. textile and apparel industries. During
the 1970s, textile and apparel industries in OECD countries achieved at
best only modest increases in output. Only in 1984 did they achieve
strong gains in imports to the United States. On the other hand, several
Third World countries with a relative abundance of labor have developed
large, rapidly growing textile and apparel industries. In 1984, according
to Department of Commerce reports, the four leading exporters of textiles and apparel to the United States—measured in million standard
yarn equivalents (SYE)—were Taiwan (1,335), Korea (1,902), Hong Kong
(1,032), and China (967). Together they accounted for 45.2 percent of all
the textile and apparel imports into the United States. The only OECD
countries in the top ten were Japan (737), Italy (506), Canada (300), and

West Germany (289). Their portion of U.S. textile and apparel imports amounted to only 10.5 percent, although exports, especially from Italy, are growing.

Two phenomena can be clearly seen in Department of Commerce figures for the apparel trade: the arrival of the NICs as a major force in the international marketplace and the changing rankings of those countries importing to the United States. In 1964, 35 percent of all apparel imports came from Japan. The next three import sources were Hong Kong, Taiwan, and the Philippines. The following ten-year period chronicles the dramatic emergence of the NICs and Japan's movement to fields requiring higher technology and promising greater rates of return. By 1974, imports from Hong Kong, Taiwan, Korea, and China accounted for 56 percent of the apparel total, while Japan's share dropped to 8 percent. During the next nine years, overall imports of apparel almost doubled, reaching 3.9 billion SYE in 1983. But imports from Hong Kong, Taiwan, and Korea more than doubled, while imports from China increased by 5,440 percent. Of total imported apparel, 69 percent of the yardage came from Hong Kong, Taiwan, Korea, and China. Japan contributed only 3 percent. New countries are continually entering the low end of the market. Imports from Sri Lanka grew from 1 million SYE in 1974 to 66 million SYE in 1983, making it the ninth ranking exporter of apparel to the United States.

A similar situation can be observed in the textile industry, though it is not yet subject to such a high level of competition from so many foreign suppliers, as it is more capital intensive than apparel. Currently, the major exporters to the U.S. market are from the most advanced tier of developing countries. Department of Commerce statistics reveal that in 1984, the major foreign suppliers of textiles besides Italy were China (up 73 percent), Taiwan (up 53 percent), Hong Kong (up 33 percent), and Japan (up 30 percent).

The reasons that textiles and apparel were among the earliest industries affected by international competition have to do with the nature of the industries themselves. The textile and apparel industries have traditionally been the means by which less developed countries begin their pursuit of industrialization. The raw materials of textile and apparel manufacture—cotton, flax, wool, ramie—are relatively common, and both textiles and apparel require less capital than most other manufactures. The low labor costs and the high percentage of direct labor involved in the production of textiles and particularly apparel make these basic industries extremely attractive, first as a source of import substitution and eventually as a primary source of export earnings with which to further economic and social development. Also, as clothing is a necessity of life, the rapid growth of the world population has created a steadily expanding market. Typically, a developing country enters developed foreign markets with low-value-added exports, but as its domestic industry grows and evolves, product lines are broadened to include manmade and synthetic fibers. The lower-value-added products in all fiber types are eventually cast off, and, in turn, become the basic exports for lower-wage-base countries.

The competitive advantage that industries in NICs possess can be illustrated by a comparison of wage scales in the apparel industry. Although labor generally accounts for less than one-third of the manufacturing cost in the apparel industry, the difference between wages in the United States and wages in developing countries is so severe that it is a major source of the developing country advantage. U.S. Department of Labor statistics show that the average wage in the U.S. apparel industry, including fringe benefits, increased from $4.00 an hour in 1975 to $6.50 an hour in 1982. During this same period, the average apparel wage, including fringe benefits, in most developing countries did not reach even $2.00 an hour. Only Hong Kong had a wage of over $2.00 an hour, and at $2.05, this hourly wage was still only 32 percent of the U.S. average. The lowest wage in a country that is a major exporter to the United States is found in China, where it is estimated that the hourly wage is $0.30, one-twentieth of the U.S. average.

The development of new technology and the transfer of technological know-how has also played an increasingly important role in the evolution of the textile and apparel industries in developing countries. At this time, industrialized countries still dominate production in areas like manmade fibers. However, production technologies of some manmade fibers are considered "mature": well established, well known, and functioning in many developing countries. As a result, fibers made from these mature-process technologies are more price competitive and more diverse in terms of production location. The same situation holds true for other textile production technology. Hong Kong, for instance, has practically turned its entire production to advanced open-end spinning and shuttleless weaving. Korea and Taiwan have been following suit. These countries are approaching rough parity with the United States in production technology.

In addition to low labor costs and in the increasing reliance on high technology, the NICs enjoy a significant advantage over the United States because of supportive trade policies. The textile and apparel markets in developing countries, particularly in the NICs, are growing, but U.S. manufacturers have only limited access to these markets. Protection of industrial goods in the Third World countries exists on all but high-priority import goods. The restrictions these countries place on imports of textile and apparels can best be understood in the context of their overall trade policy. Basically, the purpose of the trade restrictions they enact is to:

1. protect infant industries and import substitution
2. promote export industries
3. save foreign exchange

In more practical terms, the first objective generally leads to restrictions of imports of textiles and clothing items when they are produced domestically; the second objective often leads to the exemption of raw or intermediate textiles and clothing items from various restrictions if used in export production; and the third objective may lead to the restriction of clothing items as nonessential goods, owing to balance of payments considerations, and thus to the restriction of their importation.

In general, governments of the major Asian textile and apparel importers tend to protect, support, and control these industries. For instance, the Korean government enacted the Provisional Law for the Adjustment of Textile facilities in 1967 to encourage the use of new equipment. This law was replaced in 1979 by the Law for Promoting Modernization of the Textile Industry, which provided a special fund to be used to encourage specialization and integration, to obtain new technology, and to train employees. In 1980, Korea formed a semiofficial organization, the Textile Industry Federation, financed by the government and by private firms. This group is designed to help firms modernize plants and equipment as a means of helping Korea become more competitive in the world market. Because textile exports account for about one-third of Korea's foreign exchange, the government has supported this key industry, which has been organized to be self-sufficient and export-oriented. In general, the domestic market is effectively shielded from imports by nontariff barriers. Textile imports are not permitted except in the following instances:

1. imports intended for re-export
2. domestic production capabilities temporarily fully utilized
3. domestic consumption not large enough to justify local production
4. prices on imported goods so low that the material must be purchased in order for Korea to remain internationally competitive in other textile markets.

Taiwan is another country that has adopted highly restrictive policies. The Taiwanese have placed emphasis on producing high-value-added textiles and the development of a high-technology, highly integrated, export-directed industry. Almost no textiles can be imported unless they aid the local textile industry.

The Response of the Textile and Apparel Industries to the Emergence of the NICs

The exponential growth in textile and apparel imports from the NICs has posed the single most significant challenge to American manufacturers since World War II. Under the pressure of rapidly increasing imports, the balance of trade in textiles and apparel fell sharply. In 1961, the United States had a textile-apparel trade deficit of $191 million, but by 1972, the deficit had risen to $2.4 billion. Textile and apparel imports totaled $11.8 billion in 1983 and $16.5 billion in 1984. As a result, according to Department of Commerce figures, the deficit reached $13.6 billion in 1984, a 53 percent increase over 1983's record $8.9 billion deficit. Slumping exports played a small though significant role in the creation of this deficit. After 1981, when textile exports reached an all-time high of $3.5 billion, they declined 35 percent to a 1984 total of $2.2 billion. In 1984 itself, they remained basically flat, increasing by only $5 million. Exports of apparel have also dropped, from a high of $1 billion in 1981 to $638 million in 1984. This represents a decrease of 4 percent over 1983 and a 38 percent decrease since 1981. The result is that the trade deficit in textile mill products grew by 138 percent in 1984, reaching a total of $2.2 billion, while the trade deficit in apparels reached $11.4 billion in 1984, up 30 percent since 1983. In fact, in 1984, for every dollar's worth of apparel exported, nearly $19 worth was imported.

During the 1970s, however, the textile industry and, to a lesser extent, the apparel industry made significant strides in achieving the adjustment necessary to counter the increasing international competitiveness of the NICs. The textile industry responded to intensified competition in world markets by accelerating the modernization of production facilities. High levels of capital expenditures were directed increasingly toward modernization, and almost all capital appropriations were made for the adoption of new technology. For more than a hundred years, the textile industry had updated and modified existing machinery. In the 1970s, completely new technology came on-line. Open-end spinning, for instance, a relatively new technique that boosts the rate of production of yarn four times over the older ring-spinning technique, reduces the number of steps involved in manufacturing some kinds of yarn from as many as fifteen to as few as three. Fabric weaving has been done by a wooden fly shuttle moving back and forth across a loom. Shuttles propelled by air or water jets were developed. These shuttleless looms yield three times the speed, yet can produce seven to eight times the fabric because they weave wider widths. They are also safer and much quieter, better satisfying Occupational Safety and Health Administration (OSHA) regulations. The consequence of this commitment is that between 1970 and 1983, as Department of Labor statistics show, textile mills achieved an annual 3.5 percent increase in productivity versus a 2.3 percent increase for all U.S. manufacturing. These efforts were successful in reducing much of the impact of imports. The combined pressures of rising imports and increased modernization, however, did lead to a decrease in employment in the textile industry of 44 percent over the past twenty-five years. However, during the 1960s and 1970s, this drop in employment occurred gradually, and the costs of social dislocation were not significant.

The 1970s were therefore a period of productive change for the textile industry. There was a trade surplus in textiles and a steady rise in the dollar value of shipments since the low point in the 1975 recession. Shipments grew by 24 percent (adjusted for inflation), while exports doubled. Although the rise in the value of textile exports benefited from inflation, the rise in prices of textile-mill products has been less than that for industrial commodities as a whole.

Restoring the competitiveness of the apparel industry was more difficult because of the fragmented structure of the industry and the labor-intensive nature of the product. However, in the 1970s, the apparel industry began to experience a major restructuring, with the result that apparel productivity grew slightly faster than that of the industrial sector as a whole. The larger firms' share of total output grew, and the product lines produced by many apparel firms were widened and upgraded.

Despite these efforts, the apparel industry in the 1970s felt significant pressure from rising imports. Figures compiled by the American Apparel Manufacturers Association show the significant impact that imports have had on domestic apparel production. In 1958, apparel imports were less than $300 million, but by the end of 1983, imported apparel increased to $7 billion (measured in 1958 dollars). That figure represented almost 25 percent of the total wholesale value of all apparel sold in the United States. In the 1960s, the value of apparel production increased by approximately 5 percent a year, while imports increased by about 12 percent a year. In 1969, apparel production was $18 billion, and apparel imports were valued at $1.2 billion. From this point the trends changed drastically. The increase in the value of imports accelerated to

15 percent a year in the 1970s, while domestic apparel production increased by only 3.5 percent a year between 1969 and 1973 and then stopped. Apparel production has not increased beyond the 1973 level of $20.8 billion (in 1958 dollars). Since 1973, apparel imports have satisfied all additional consumer demand for apparel.

Textiles and Apparel in the 1980s

The surge of imports during the 1980s undermined much of the progress achieved in the previous decade and created the sense of crisis that infuses the industry today. At the same time, U.S. textile and apparel manufacturers had to contend with the effects of worldwide recession. Demand in the United States intensified in recent years, especially when compared to the relatively sluggish demand in other developed nations. U.S. apparel consumption (measured in equivalent square yards of fabric) rose by 5.8 percent in 1981 and by 2.4 percent in 1982, following declines in each of the preceding two years. Thanks to massive inventory rebuilding by retailers, consumption increased by 11 percent in 1983, though it has moderated since then. This development has made the United States a magnet for imports from countries with low-wage scales. It is currently estimated that one out of every three garments sold in the United States was manufactured overseas. Much higher ratios are prevalent for most types of sweaters; for women's cotton slacks and shorts; for women's cotton knit shirts, blouses, and woven shirts; for cotton skirts; for women's cotton coats and playsuits; and for men's and boys' cotton coats, including suit-type coats. The domestic apparel industry has remained relatively strong in hosiery, underwear, night wear, and robes and dressing gowns. It produced 96 percent of these units on the domestic market in 1973, which, measured in terms of dollar value, represented 98 percent of the market. By 1983, these figures had fallen only to 90 and 92 percent, respectively. Nonetheless, in 1984 the total apparel trade deficit reached $11.4 billion, an increase of 43 percent over 1983. By 1984, apparel imports had increased to $12 billion. Apparel imports in the first quarter of 1985 were running at rate 10 percent higher than in 1984.

Despite the recession and the influx of imports, profits in apparels in 1982 held near the 1981 level of 3.4 percent of sales. An abatement in material cost increases, lower interest expenses, and in some cases improved cash positions as a result of asset liquidations helped bolster profits. Overall profits showed some improvement in 1983, partially because of a resurgence in consumer demand for work and casual clothes, which are generally produced in large-volume runs.

The textile industry entered the 1980s in a better position than the apparel industry, but it too was hard hit by a surge in imports. Imports of textile products became much more extensive and are growing at a sharply accelerating rate. Since 1981, imports have exceeded exports, and they are now a factor in such areas as home furnishings. The value of imports in 1984 totaled $4.5 billion, up 40 percent, and the textile trade deficit rose by 138 percent, to $2.3 billion. The major foreign suppliers of textiles were Italy (up 75 percent), China (up 73 percent), Taiwan (up 53 percent), Hong Kong (up 33 percent), and Japan (up 30 percent). The increase in imports from Italy is part of a surge of shipments from uncontrolled sources, including the European Economic Community. Imports had reached $6.2 billion for the year as of May 1985.

The Role of International Exchange Rates

The rapid increase in the value of the dollar during the first half of the 1980s is a major factor in the deteriorating U.S. trade position in textiles and apparel. There has, however, been significant debate on the extent to which the rise of the dollar has affected the industry. A recently completed study prepared by Economic Consulting Services concluded that "virtually all apparel import growth and much of textile import growth from low-wage countries was not related to the U.S. dollar appreciation." This conclusion was based on a survey of the twenty-five largest country suppliers to the United States. The authors of this report found that aggregate U.S. imports of apparel and textiles from countries whose currencies have depreciated significantly against the dollar between 1981 and 1984 were only slightly higher than imports from countries with stable rates of exchange. A further breakdown of the major supplying countries experiencing depreciation against the U.S. dollar revealed significant differences between higher and low-wage countries. Imports of both textiles and apparel from the low-wage developing countries rose less rapidly than imports from the six countries with relatively stable exchange rates and much less rapidly than imports of textiles and apparels from the five European countries among our major suppliers and from Canada.

Objections can be raised to this study, however. The authors consider wage scale as a sole measure of competitiveness, at the expense of other measures like unit production cost, and they assume as a norm the textile and apparel imports from six nations, only one of which, Taiwan, is a significant exporter of textiles and apparel. In 1984, Taiwan accounted for 13.6 percent of U.S. imports (measured in million SYE), while the other five countries, Singapore, Dominican Republic, Malaysia, Egypt, and Haiti, together accounted for only 5.0 percent. The authors admit that the price of the dollar had some impact—possibly a major one— on imports from Hong Kong, Korea, Italy, Pakistan, Canada, West Germany, Mexico, Indonesia, India, the Philippines, Brazil, the United Kingdom, France, and Spain. Although the growth of imports from these places may be small compared to the growth of imports from countries with small textile and apparel industries, they accounted for 52 percent of 1984 imports, according to Department of Commerce figures.

No matter how they judge its importance, most observers agree that the rise in price of the dollar has been an important impetus in the rising U.S. trade deficit in textiles and apparel. Although the apparel and textile industries had long shown a negative trade balance, the appreciation of the dollar led that deficit to increase at an unprecedented rate. The longer the dollar remains high, the more serious these effects become. Although the dollar began its rise in value in 1981, there was a lag time of approximately eighteen months to two years before the apparel and textile markets reflected this growth. Between 1982 and 1983, for instance, textile imports rose by 14.9 percent and apparel imports rose by 17.4 percent. In the next year, however, textile imports rose by 47.2 percent, while apparel imports rose by 44.7 percent. The effects of the overvalued dollar on U.S. exports of textiles and apparel are more immediate. In 1982, exports of apparel abruptly dropped by 25 percent, after increasing gradually since 1971. A similar phenomenon was observable in textile exports, which fell by 24 percent in 1981, after having risen since 1976. The overvalued dollar also shifted market emphasis from other OECD countries to the U.S. market, further increasing competition.

The consequences of the strengthening of the dollar on industries with low profit margins, like textiles and apparel, are long-term. When the dollar was not overvalued, as in the 1970s, the textile industry performed strongly, and segments of the apparel industry showed strength as well. In a three-year period in the late 1970s, finished apparel exports doubled. Apparel-industry representatives argue that had those exchange rates prevailed, the U.S. apparel industry would have found a significant new market for U.S.-made apparel. Although the dollar has dropped in relation to our OECD trading partners, it has not dropped significantly against the NICs. If the dollar should turn around, it will take several years to reestablish these markets, if they can be regained at all. Furthermore, because the profit margin in textiles and apparels is low, even small increases in the value of the dollar can cause firms that would have otherwise remained vigorous to fail.

The Retailing Industry and the Changing Market for Apparel

Apparel sales constitute the most important merchandise category for department stores, mass merchandisers, and specialty stores. These stores in turn provide the principal outlet for the apparel produced in the United States. About one-third of the apparel sold in the United States is sold through specialty stores. This ratio, however, is expected to decline somewhat in the coming years. In fact, during the past decade there has been a slight contraction in the number of stores specializing in apparel and accessories. Department of Commerce statistics show that retail sales by apparel and accessory stores dropped from 5.3 percent of total retail sales in 1973 to 4.5 percent in 1984. Department stores are believed to account for approximately one-fifth of all apparel retail sales, with about one-third of this volume accounted for by about twenty high-growth stores. These stores have been increasing their market share and will likely continue to do so. Slightly more than one-fifth of all apparel sales are attributed to the four large national chains: Sears, J.C.Penney, K Mart, and Montgomery Ward. Among the other outlets, off-price retailers are believed to be selling less than 5 percent of all apparel, but the ratio is expected to double, roughly, over the balance of the current decade.

Retailing bounced back sharply from the 1982 recession as rising employment and personal income led to an accelerated rate of consumer spending. Department stores and the national chains expanded their combined sales by 7.9 percent in 1983, following a modest 3 percent rise in 1982. Retail sales continued steady until the second half of 1984, when erratically lower consumer spending hit general merchandisers particularly hard. Erring on the side of optimism, department-store managements generally made substantial inventory commitments for the key Christmas quarter, extrapolating future sales trends from the buoyant demand in the early months of 1984, rather than risk losing sales for lack of merchandise. When anticipated holiday buying failed to materialize—reflecting unfavorable weather, the uncertainty created by the Treasury Department tax-reform proposals, and a slowdown in the rise of spendable income—retailers found themselves with excess merchandise on hand. While sales increased by 11.2 percent for the top fifteen general-merchandise retailers in 1984, their profits rose by only 2.7 percent, and net profit margins slipped to 3.6 percent of sales, from 3.9 percent in 1983.

Entering 1985, the situation was mixed. A leaner inventory posture paid off for major department-store retailers in the quarter ended April 30, 1985. Aided by the absence of large markdowns, Associated Dry Goods, Federated, Allied, May Department Stores, and Dayton Hudson reported robust earnings gains on modest sales increases, even on top of strong year-earlier gains. However, excess inventories continued to squeeze earnings of other national chains. In June 1985, retail apparel sales rose by 2 percent to a new high, despite a fall in overall retail sales. Retail sales remained sluggish in July but increased dramatically in August, by 1.7 percent. Sales of apparel were an important factor.

According to a recently released report by the Marketing Science Institute, over the next five years growth is expected to be sluggish in general merchandise sales. General merchandise retailers are expected to increase sales volume by about 2.4 percent per year after inflation, compared with the average annual increases of 4.9 percent between 1967 and 1980. Moreover, apparel sales are predicted to slow to a crawl, maintaining an annual per-capita sales growth of only 0.8 percent per year through 1990. The reasons for this gloomy forecast are projections of a slight reduction in disposable personal income as a percentage of GNP and, more important, a decline in the proportion of income Americans will choose to spend on general merchandise and services.

Another contributing factor to the problems that will face retailers in the coming years is an excess of selling space. Profitability per square foot has remained the same or dropped lower than levels in the mid-1970s. Part of this is the result of the drop in per-capita spending on apparel and on all general merchandise since the mid-1970s. Another factor has been the 200 percent growth in shopping-space square footage between 1972 and 1984, as reported by *Shopping Center World*. Overstoring is the legacy of the aggressive expansion strategies launched by many leading chains in pursuit of greater market share—strategies that persisted well into the 1970s despite the saturation of many major markets.

To cope with small growth and overstoring, retailers are vacating marginal locations; scrutinizing divisional returns on investment more systematically to improve allocation of corporate resources; and consolidating or, when warranted, shedding divisions. In recent years, major retailers have eliminated whole divisions—F.W. Woolworth terminated its unprofitable Woolco operations, while J.C. Penney withdrew from household durables and automotive businesses. Strategies to strengthen expense ratios by paring payroll, energy, and interest costs have also been implemented. In addition, managements are devoting enormous sums to marketing and management information systems, while searching for "niche" businesses to serve as growth vehicles in the years ahead.

A related strategy is the reliance on labels as merchandising tools. In recent years, apparel retailers have increased their purchases of private-label merchandise and will probably continue this practice in the years ahead. The basic reasons for this practice are to counter apparel designers who are in the process of starting their own free-standing and in-store boutiques; to offer a choice between designer-made garments and merchandise that reflects a store's originality; and to maintain a desired markup. Initial efforts were directed toward providing basic garments, but favorable customer reaction and encouragement has led to the creation of selections that are more stylized and fashion-oriented. In prior years, private-label manufacturing sources were located in the Far East, but some sources have now shifted to England, Italy, and France. Although production costs are higher in Europe, quality control is reported excellent, and on-time delivery is assured. Suppliers also find customers in those countries more receptive to domestic shipment. Other firms combine in-house labels with designer labels. J.C. Penney's addition of Levi Strauss lines under its trade-up program, for example, enjoyed considerable success. Penney also developed its own labels of Gentry, Hunt Club, and Fox. It has also added lines from Halston and Lee Wright on exclusive contracts. Despite these efforts, retailers are very concerned about their ability to continue to generate profits on apparel sales.

The Current Situation

Despite the harrowing economic conditions that textile and apparel manufacturers faced in the early 1980s, they have continued to pursue their goal of adjustment. Recently, capital spending by apparel companies has begun to be used to improve productivity, rather than merely to expand facilities. *Industry Week* reported that in 1984, the productivity of the apparel industry increased by 4.0 percent annually, 1.2 percent more than for all manufacturing, as a result of the introduction of automation. In addition to increasing productivity, technological innovation has the effect of reducing the response time to new trends in the industry, which is particularly important in a fashion-dependent industry like apparel. The process of automating the apparel industry, however, is hampered by the small size of its typical operations. Most apparel companies do not generate a sufficient return on investment to attract the capital necessary to underwrite these improvements. Laser-based cutting and stitching machines, microcomputer controls, and robots are out of reach of all but the largest and most financially secure corporations.

However, a Standard & Poor's tabulation of fifteen major companies showed a profit decline of almost 8 percent in the first half of 1984, which stemmed from excess inventories in the distribution pipeline, coupled with sharply higher apparel imports. Furthermore, although apparels registered a slight gain in employment in 1984 in response to the upturn in the economy, in the first half of 1985 this trend was reversed.

Textile manufacturers have similarly continued their efforts to modernize. According to figures in the *Survey of Current Business*, in the first quarter of 1985 the textile industry invested $2.0 billion (adjusted at annual rates). This is approximately a 33 percent increase over 1983, and it occurred in a quarter when overall manufacturing investment declined by 0.4 percent. Investment rose by 23.0 percent in 1984 alone, exceeding the average increase in the manufacturing sector by 4 percent.

Nonetheless, performance declined sharply through the first half of 1985. Inventory accumulation and a substantial increase in imports were factors in the slowing of textile activity. Figures for 1985 showed shipments decreasing by 4.7 percent, yet preliminary figures for 1986 suggest an increase of approximately 4 percent, reversing the 1985 trend but remaining below 1984 levels. Profits plummeted by over 55 percent in the first quarter of 1985, while textile production slumped by 1.2 percent in May. As of June 1985, the Bureau of Labor Statistics reported that total textile employment had declined to an all-time low of 699,000, of which 603,000 were production workers. This represented a decrease in total employment of 7 percent since June 1984, and it was attributable to a closing of plants. According to figures in *Textile World*, there were seventy-eight plant closings in 1984 and thirty-three plant closings in the first half of 1985.

A *Wall Street Journal* survey revealed that in the second half of 1985, after-tax profits of 425 industrial companies registered a 21 percent profit slump over the previous year. The textile industry, hurt by a sharp rise in imports and a decline in demand for fabrics from retailers, registered a 55 percent drop in net income after taxes. The apparel industry registered a 13 percent increase, but this figure was distorted by a 400 percent increase in profits turned in by Levi Strauss.

Members of the textile and apparel industries, as well as representatives of the retailing industry, are approaching the coming decade with some apprehension. There is wide agreement on the need to streamline operations and to improve cooperation along the production chain, but there is also a widespread feeling that despite the major steps taken to improve productivity and to achieve adjustment, the recent sudden surge in imports and the resulting decline in profit margins allow little leeway for the reconciliation of their conflicting interests and no time to continue the adjustment process.

There has been growing impatience, particularly among leaders in the textile and apparel industries, with the present administration's handling of the import crisis. In a speech before the South Carolina Textile Manufacturers Association, American Textile Manufacturers Institute president Ellison McKissick, Jr., termed the Reagan administrations's textile trade policies "absolutely, utterly ineffective." The textile and apparel industries lobbied strongly for the textile trade bill, S. 680 and H.R. 1562, which was vetoed by President Reagan.

Table 2–1
Average Hourly Earnings of Production Workers in Selected Apparel and Knitting Industries, 1950–1984

Year	Manufacturing		Textile Mill Products		Apparel and Related Products					
	Total	Nondurable	Total SIC #22	Knit Outerwear Mills #2253	Total SIC #23	M&B Suits and Coats #231	M&B Furnishings #232	WM&J Outerwear #233	WG&J Underwear #234	GC&J Outerwear #236
1950	1.44	1.35	1.23	1.13	1.24	1.34	0.99	1.51	1.06	1.09
1955	1.85	1.67	1.38	1.39	1.37	1.61	1.13	1.58	1.25	1.25
1960	2.26	2.05	1.61	1.60	1.59	1.85	1.33	1.77	1.45	1.46
1965	2.61	2.36	1.87	1.88	1.83	2.16	1.54	2.02	1.64	1.67
1970	3.35	3.08	2.45	2.47	2.39	2.91	2.10	2.57	2.18	2.23
1975	4.83	4.37	3.42	3.35	3.17	3.84	2.86	3.23	2.90	2.94
1976	5.22	4.70	3.69	3.55	3.40	4.10	3.09	3.45	3.11	3.12
1977	5.68	5.11	3.99	3.72	3.62	4.41	3.27	3.65	3.28	3.28
1978	6.17	5.53	4.30	3.94	3.94	4.79	3.58	3.92	3.57	3.54
1979	6.70	6.01	4.66	4.27	4.23	5.11	3.90	4.22	3.86	3.84
1980	7.27	6.55	5.07	4.69	4.56	5.34	4.23	4.61	4.15	4.20
1981	7.99	7.18	5.52	5.05	4.97	5.72	4.57	4.95	4.52	4.56
1982	8.49	7.74	5.82	5.26	5.20	6.00	4.78	5.13	4.71	4.74
1983	8.83	8.08	6.18	5.52	5.37	6.21	4.93	5.31	4.89	4.80
1984	9.17	8.37	6.46	5.78	5.53	6.50	5.08	5.48	5.07	4.95

Source: *Employment and Earnings*, Bureau of Labor Statistics.

Table 2–2
Capital Expenditures on New Plant and Equipment, 1972–1982
(millions of dollars)

SIC Code	Industry Description	1972	1974	1976	1978	1980	1982
23	Apparel and related products	442	391	423	514	608	673
231	M&B suits and coats	35	28	25	26	30	25
232	M&B furnishings	121	107	100	138	180	157
2321	Shirts and nightwear	31	27	32	43	43	37
2327	Separate trousers	23	29	28	27	21	36
2328	Work clothing	23	35	26	41	87	57
2329	Other clothing NEC	14	11	10	24	15	18
233	WMJ outerwear	124	97	128	130	166	222
2331	Blouses	10	14	18	27	34	29
2335	Dresses	67	44	60	38	51	68
2337	Suits, coats, and skirts	24	19	28	22	29	39
2339	Other outerwear NEC	23	21	23	43	52	86
234	W&C underwear	25	18	21	28	35	38
2341	W&C underwear	20	14	15	22	29	31
2342	Corsets and allied garments	5	4	6	6	6	7
236	C&I outerwear	13	14	14	14	21	31
2361	Dresses and blouses	5	5	8	7	7	12
2363	Coats and suits	1	1	2	1	2	2
2369	Other outerwear NEC	8	8	4	6	12	17
2384	Robes and dressing gowns	2	2	2	10	6	4

		1,083	1,170	1,087	1,356	1,495	1,570
22	Textile mill products						
225	Knit apparel mills only	100	78	73	104	120	120
2251	Women's hosiery except socks	21	14	13	23	28	25
2252	Hosiery NEC	17	12	15	15	22	32
2253	Knit outerwear mills	53	42	35	44	49	53
2254	Knit underwear mills	9	10	10	22	21	9

Source: 1982 Census of Manufacturers and Annual Survey of Manufacturers.

Table 2–3
Textile Mill Production, 1973–1982
(1967 = 100)

Year	Textile Mill Products						Industrial Production
	Fabrics			Knit Goods	Carpeting	Total	
	Cotton	Manmade	Wool				
1982	60.2	172.1	47.7	172.3	182.0	124.5	138.6
R1981	66.1	198.9	52.3	186.6	186.2	135.7	151.0
R1980	73.6	191.1	55.0	180.7	203.2	138.6	147.0
1979	74.9	186.4	55.4	191.4	222.0	145.0	152.5
1978	73.4	172.1	57.3	183.4	184.1	137.5	146.1
1977	76.5	163.3	49.6	186.3	181.6	134.4	138.2
1976	80.8	161.1	41.9	185.3	166.3	134.6	130.5
1975	70.7	141.0	44.8	175.0	157.7	122.3	117.8
1974	76.6	158.4	44.8	183.5	179.9	132.8	129.3
1973	83.5	162.6	56.0	194.0	194.3	142.9	129.8

Source: Federal Reserve Board.
R = revised.

Table 2–4
Business Failures in Textile and Apparel Industries, 1960–1983

Year	Total U.S. No.	Total U.S. Liability $1,000	Total Manufacturing and Mining No.	Total Manufacturing and Mining Liability $1,000	Total Textiles and Apparel No.	Total Textiles and Apparel Liability $1,000	Total Textiles Mill Products No.	Total Textiles Mill Products Liability $1,000	Total Apparel and Related Products No.	Total Apparel and Related Products Liability $1,000
1960	15,445	938,630	2,612	289,635	435	36,374	70	7,053	363	29,321
1965	13,514	1,321,666	2,097	350,324	317	39,128	44	6,472	273	32,656
1970	10,748	1,887,754	2,035	817,841	311	105,520	69	40,163	242	65,357
1972	9,566	2,000,244	1,576	766,991	247	80,532	42	25,234	205	55,298
1973	9,345	2,298,606	1,463	797,490	213	130,957	40	47,493	173	83,464
1974	9,915	3,053,137	1,557	833,824	301	230,823	83	122,710	218	108,113
1975	11,432	4,380,170	1,645	1,020,609	292	112,901	65	48,177	227	64,724
1976	9,628	3,011,271	1,360	1,121,722	196	220,659	51	167,548	145	53,111
1977	7,919	3,095,317	1,122	1,221,122	173	520,302	36	425,334	137	94,968
1978	6,619	2,656,006	1,013	878,727	134	96,451	40	50,161	94	46,290
1979	7,564	2,667,362	1,165	970,178	162	125,077	38	42,949	124	82,128
1980	11,742	4,635,080	1,599	1,885,017	185	143,327	51	68,059	134	75,268
1981	16,794	6,955,180	2,224	2,370,415	215	314,205	57	162,378	158	151,827
1982	24,908	15,610,792	3,683	5,509,902	284	313,537	59	116,801	225	196,736
1983	31,334	16,072,860	4,433	6,371,932	316	245,750	66	69,668	250	176,082

Table 2–4 continued

Year	Total Manufacturing and Mining	% of Total U.S. Failures			% of Total Manufacturing and Mining Failures		
		Textile and Apparel			Textile and Apparel		
		Total	Textile	Apparel	Total	Textile	Apparel
1960	16.9	2.8	0.5	2.3	16.7	2.7	13.9
1965	15.5	2.3	0.3	2.0	15.1	2.1	13.0
1970	18.9	2.9	0.6	2.3	15.3	3.4	11.9
1972	16.5	2.5	0.4	2.1	15.7	2.7	13.0
1973	15.6	2.3	0.4	1.9	14.5	2.7	11.8
1974	15.7	3.0	0.8	2.2	19.3	5.3	14.0
1975	14.4	2.6	0.6	2.0	17.8	4.0	13.8
1976	14.1	2.0	0.5	1.5	14.4	3.8	10.6
1977	14.2	2.2	0.5	1.7	15.4	3.2	12.2
1978	15.3	2.0	0.6	1.4	13.2	3.9	9.3
1979	15.4	2.1	0.5	1.6	13.9	3.3	10.6
1980	13.6	1.6	0.4	1.2	11.6	3.2	8.4
1981	13.2	1.3	0.3	1.0	9.7	2.6	7.1
1982	14.8	1.1	0.2	0.9	7.7	1.6	6.1
1983	14.1	1.0	0.2	0.8	7.1	1.5	5.6

Source: Dun & Bradstreet, Inc. This record includes those businesses that ceased operations following assignment or bankruptcy; ceased loss to creditors after such actions as execution, foreclosure, or attachment; voluntarily withdrew leaving unpaid obligations; were involved in court actions such as receivership, reorganization, or arrangement; or voluntarily compromised with creditors.

Table 2–5
U.S. Imports of Cotton, Wool, and Manmade Fiber Apparel from Selected Countries, 1964–1984
(millions of SYE)

	1964	1968	1974	1978	1980	1982	1983	1984
Hong Kong	168	321	369	695	628	690	761	815
Taiwan	36	148	422	608	670	748	867	936
Korea	11	144	294	458	494	576	643	684
China	0	0	8	63	166	357	430	444
Subtotal	215	613	1,093	1,824	1,958	2,371	2,701	2,879
% of total	38%	53%	56%	63%	68%	70%	69%	61%
Japan	197	313	164	170	82	76	96	138
% of total	35%	27%	8%	6%	3%	2%	3%	3%
Philippines	44	43	102	158	148	161	177	234
India	—	—	27	77	69	73	106	131
Indonesia	—	—	—	—	5	38	46	129
Singapore	—	23	90	85	71	82	89	128
Sri Lanka	—	—	1	10	43	59	66	108
Thailand	—	—	42	46	35	53	66	106
Dominican Republic	—	—	6	35	59	76	76	94
Mexico	—	13	91	91	92	56	60	86
Haiti	—	—	41	53	58	54	60	68
Macao	—	—	12	37	43	43	50	61
Subtotal	—	—	412	592	623	695	793	1,145
% of total	—	—	21%	20%	21%	20%	20%	24%

Table 2–5 continued

	1964	1968	1974	1978	1980	1982	1983	1984
All other countries	—	—	268	315	221	240	297	560
% of total	—	—	15%	11%	8%	8%	8%	12%
Total all countries	561	1,153	1,937	2,901	2,884	3,382	3,894	4,722
	100%	100%	100%	100%	100%	100%	100%	100%

Source: Office of Textiles and Apparel, U.S. Department of Commerce.

Table 2–6
U.S. Imports, Exports, and Trade Balance of Apparel and Textile Mill Products, 1967–1984
(millions of dollars)

Year	Apparel			Textile Mill Products			Apparel/Textile Trade Balance
	Imports	Exports	Balance	Imports	Exports	Balance	
1967	595	119	− 476	804	509	− 295	− 771
1968	786	131	− 655	929	501	− 428	− 1,083
1969	1,013	164	− 849	1,007	550	− 457	− 1,306
1970	1,053	155	− 998	1,122	578	− 544	− 1,542
1971	1,402	164	− 1,238	1,359	607	− 752	− 1,990
1972	1,718	198	− 1,520	1,497	745	− 752	− 2,272
1973	1,956	229	− 1,727	1,541	1,164	− 377	− 2,104
1974	2,095	333	− 1,762	1,597	1,704	+ 107	− 1,655
1975	2,318	341	− 1,977	1,212	1,533	+ 321	− 1,656
1976	3,257	434	− 2,823	1,626	1,855	+ 229	− 2,594
1977	3,650	524	− 3,126	1,765	1,857	+ 92	− 3,034
1978	4,833	548	− 4,285	2,212	2,073	− 139	− 4,424
1979	5,015	772	− 4,243	2,214	3,029	+ 815	− 3,428
1980	5,703	1,001	− 4,702	2,475	3,458	+ 983	− 3,719
1981	6,756	1,032	− 5,724	3,015	3,474	+ 459	− 5,265
1982	7,386	775	− 6,611	2,772	2,650	− 122	− 6,733
1983	8,649	664	− 7,985	3,167	2,241	− 926	− 8,911
1984	12,029	638	− 11,391	4,451	2,246	− 2,205	− 13,596

Source: Office of Textiles and Apparel, Department of Commerce.

Table 2–7
Effect of Exchange Rate on Comparison of Unit Labor Costs, 1979 and 1985
(U.S. = 100)

	1979[a]	1985[b]
United States	100	100
West Germany	193	119
France	157	101
United Kingdom	141	90
Japan	101	61

[a]1979 average.
[b]January 1985.

Table 2–8
Real Effective Exchange Rates in Selected Industrial and Developing Countries, 1980–1985
(index numbers, 1980–1982 average = 100)

	Industrial Countries								Developing Countries			
	United States	Canada	Japan	Australia	France	Germany	Italy	United Kingdom	Hong Kong	Indonesia	Korea	Taiwan
1980	89.4	99.6	103.0	93.0	102.1	103.5	103.5	99.9	99.5	88.4	97.8	101.6
1981	100.6	100.0	104.6	102.7	100.1	97.3	98.7	102.3	98.9	99.8	100.3	101.8
1982	109.9	100.4	92.3	104.3	97.8	99.2	97.8	97.9	101.6	111.7	101.9	96.6
1983	112.7	103.1	96.6	100.0	96.1	99.3	100.1	92.0	95.8	96.3	97.6	94.5
1984	118.2	101.2	97.6	105.1	96.8	96.5	101.1	89.3	100.2	96.9	96.5	97.0
1985	121.3	97.3	96.4	89.2	99.6	95.4	99.7	91.9	104.2	95.8	89.2	94.6

Source: Morgan Guaranty Trust Company, *World Financial Markets.*

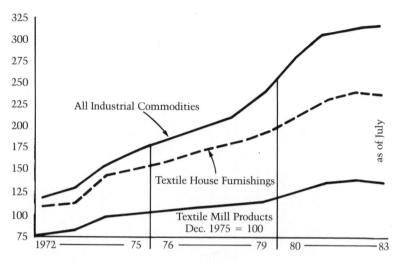

Source: Bureau of Labor Statistics.
1967 = 100.

Figure 2–1. Producer Price Indexes, 1972–1983

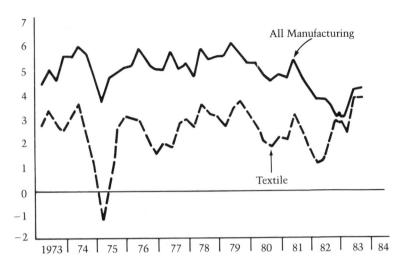

Source: Federal Trade Commission.
Quarterly—as percent of sales.

Figure 2–2. Textile Earnings, 1973–1984

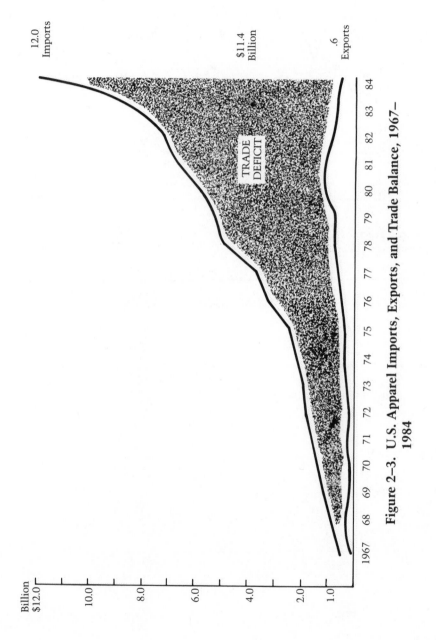

Figure 2–3. U.S. Apparel Imports, Exports, and Trade Balance, 1967–1984

3
Declining Competitiveness in the OECD: A Comparison with the United States and Japan

The trade surpluses that European countries are currently enjoying create a misleading impression of their international competitiveness. In fact, although U.S. competitiveness has dropped sharply during the 1970s and 1980s as a consequence of a myriad of factors, including the emergence of the NICs and the rise in the value of the dollar, the United States has performed relatively well in comparison to its European counterparts. Between 1970 and 1982, GNP in the United States increased at an annual average rate of 2.6 percent, according to figures from *International Financial Statistics.* Germany, the United Kingdom, and Italy lagged behind that figure, while France grew at 3.0 percent. Since the beginning of the recovery in 1982, America's gains in real GNP have far outstripped increases in Europe. Gross domestic product (GDP) grew by 3.7 percent in 1983 and 6.8 percent in 1984, while neither Germany, France, the United Kingdom, nor Italy achieved a growth rate of more than 2.9 percent between 1982 and 1985. In the first quarter of 1985, real GNP in Germany was down and the GNP in France showed no gain. Performance in the United States, though hardly strong, was better than that of its European counterparts.

Other indicators reinforce the impression that European competitiveness has fallen more than that of the United States. The Europeans, despite strenuous efforts, have not appreciably improved the levels of employment since 1970, whereas the U.S. economy has added 30 million jobs during the same period. Unemployment rates for Western Europe as a whole have doubled since 1980, while unemployment in the United States, after rising sharply, has dropped back to 7 percent, slightly higher than its level in 1980. The United States has also achieved greater gains in industrial production than its European counterparts. In the second half of the 1970s, OECD figures show that U.S. production rose twice as fast as European production, and that since the end of the recession, it has chalked up even more substantial gains. It has logged a growth of 21 percent since 1982. During the same period, the Germans registered an 11 percent gain, while French industrial output has remained the same since late 1983. Using 1980 as a base line, the figures for Europe are even more dismal. At the end of the first quarter of 1985, Italy, France, and Germany were producing at the same level they had been in 1980. Of the large industrial nations, only the United Kingdom had registered a significant increase, up 6 percent. During the same period, industrial production in the United States had risen by 14 percent.

The U.S. economy has performed well compared to that of the European nations, even though the United States and the European nations experienced comparable problems in the international marketplace. According to Department of Commerce figures, since 1970 the import share of the U.S. domestic market more than doubled, from 8 percent to a little under 19 percent. During the same period, the share of the European Community (EC) internal market for manufactures claimed by suppliers outside the Community rose from 11 percent to 17 percent.

The Europeans have attempted to strengthen the performance of their industrial sector in several ways. The European governments have made substantial efforts, especially since the second oil shock, to put their economic houses in order. Measures have been taken to foster structural adjustments designed to increase labor-market flexibility, to encourage innovative small and medium-sized industries, to privatize functions ill-suited to the public sector, and to curb budget deficits so as to lower interest rates and boost investment. But despite these efforts, European governments have not been successful in stimulating domestic demand, which is presently stagnant across much of Continental Europe. Germany's domestic manufacturing orders were almost flat in the first part of 1985 in comparison to both late-1984 and year-earlier levels. And in many countries, retail sales in early 1985, measured in volume, were only slightly above the levels of September 1984.

The Europeans have been more successful in minimizing the effect of the flood of imports from low-wage suppliers. Their principal strategy has been to increase export trade with the United States. The salient factor, of course, that has made this strategy possible is the appreciation of the dollar. According to figures compiled by Morgan Guaranty Trust, in the first ten months of 1984, exports to the United States from Western Europe grew by 31.6 percent and represented 1.9 percent of total Western European GNP. The growth in U.S. trade has allowed European nations to reduce or eliminate current account deficits. In fact, in the cases of France and Germany, exports played a major role in the growth of GNP in 1984. Recent statistics show that exports continue strong. In Germany, for example, during the first four months of 1985, the volume of foreign manufacturing orders rose by 4.6 percent over late-1984 levels, marking up a twelve-month increase of 13 percent.

The expectation that U.S. imports can be relied on to sustain world economic performance, however, may be a mistaken one. The dollar must depreciate further in the near term; otherwise, pressure in the United States to limit imports will become even more widespread. There are now an estimated three hundred bills pending before the United States Congress, all aimed at curbing foreign imports. Because European economic growth is so heavily dependent on U.S. markets remaining open, protectionist measures taken in the United States could virtually eliminate the relatively small gains in GNP that EEC countries have managed to chalk up in recent years.

Furthermore, trade with the United States has created the potential for serious structural problems in the manufacturing sector. Dependency on this trade has led to increased production in such industries as consumer electronics, which could be disastrous if trade with the United States is sharply curtailed. Because other industrialized countries have not recovered strongly from the 1982 recession, there are few secondary markets for these products. Furthermore, rising export earnings mask such important realities as the declining competitiveness of European nations in other international markets during the last fifteen years; the increase in import penetration in European markets; and the significant retrenchment in many industrial sectors which the first two factors have precipitated. The situation of the textile and apparel industries in selected OECD countries illustrates this point.

The Case of the Textile and Apparel Industries in West Germany, Italy, the United Kingdom, and France

In the years following World War II, the European nations had highly advanced textile industries, and several countries were acknowledged trendsetters in apparel design and production. However, after enjoying years of prosperity, employment in the European textile and apparel industries began to drop in the 1960s and early 1970s, and by 1974 most European governments realized that restructuring of the industry was necessary. As in the United States, the apparel industry was the first to feel the effects of increased competition from abroad. The strategy that many Europeans adopted was to press for time to allow for adjustment to the new economic conditions. To secure this transitional period, they sought temporary protection. Rather than attempt the negotiation of many bilateral trade treaties, the European Community accepted the Multifiber Arrangement. They also sought to identify the strengths and weaknesses within their own textile industries and tried to concentrate on strengthening those sectors holding the greatest comparative advantages. They sought to transfer individuals from uncompetitive textile industry segments into specialized components of the industry or into other industries.

One measure used to promote restructuring of the apparel industry was to support or encourage firms exporting finished component parts or semifinished manufactures to lower-cost countries for completion. The finished products were then reexported for distribution. This strategy was relied on extensively in Germany. Other responses, used in both textiles and apparel, were import substitution, industrial development assistance, and export assistance. It is important to keep in mind, however, that these actions were not purely a response to pressure from the international market. They also reflected pressure from interest groups such as manufacturers and labor unions. Although it is difficult to generalize from the results, it is fair to say that on the average, measures designed to encourage textile and apparel firms to compete against the same items in which developing countries specialized were misdirected. The most successful adjustments were made in countries where retrenchment in certain sectors was accompanied by specialization, emphasis on flexibility, and attention to the market.

The consequences of this adjustment in the textile and apparel industries can be easily seen in declining production and a shrinking work force. From 1973 to 1983, all countries with the exception of Italy had experienced a decline in production. The United Kingdom was producing at only 60 percent of its 1973 levels. Production also fell in France and Germany. During the same period, OECD figures revealed that employment had dropped substantially. In the United Kingdom, jobs fell by 240,000, while France and Germany lost 40 percent of their work force. However, the restructuring that resulted led to mixed performances. Since 1973, Germany and Italy have recorded substantial gains in productivity, while gains in France and the United Kingdom have lagged behind.

By and large, one reason that textile industries in Europe fared so poorly in the 1960s and 1970s was that they were late in recognizing the potential of the international marketplace. They tended to depend on their often fragmented, relatively high-cost, labor-intensive, low-profit domestic apparel industries to absorb a major portion of their output. This dependency increasingly became a strategic weakness as the apparel industries of developing countries ventured out into the international market and dampened the performance of the OECD apparel sector. The comparative advantages enjoyed by developing countries because of lower labor costs, augmented by the rapid and relatively easy transfer of apparel-manufacturing technology, neutralized in many instances the productivity gains achieved by mills in developed countries. The result has been not only a significant penetration by developing countries into the domestic apparel markets of OECD nations but substantial strain on the OECD textile industry as well.

The relative strengths of the Western European textile and apparel industries can be measured by examining their performance on the international marketplace. During the years between 1969 and 1982, there has been a steadily increasing trade surplus in textiles and an inexorable rise in the apparel trade deficit. OECD figures reveal, however, sharp differences among countries. Italy has always been a net exporter of textiles and apparel, while France and the United Kingdom have deficits in both these areas.

Country-by-Country Analysis of the Textile and
Apparel Industries in West Germany, Italy, the
United Kingdom, and France

West Germany. During the period of reconstruction that followed World War II, the German textile and apparel industries benefited from a massive inflow of labor and from pent-up consumer demand. The 1950s was a period of substantial growth, but in the 1960s, imports increased dramatically and employment started to decline. This long-term trend appeared relatively early in West Germany, in comparison to other EC countries. The change in trend, as indeed the whole adjustment process, with its accompanying rapid decline in the number of firms, can be directly related to two factors. First, Germany had adopted a free-market position in relation to the textile and apparel sectors. It pursued a fairly liberal import policy within the margin permitted by the EEC. Furthermore, the West German government offered no specific sectoral support of the kind seen in other countries. Second, increasing pressure of industry-wide minimum wages began to exceed the productivity potential in many segments of the textile and apparel sectors.

The responses adopted by the industry to mounting competition from low-cost textile suppliers can be divided into two periods. Up until 1970, the textile industry in Germany, like that in many other countries, saw its future in capital-intensive mass production of a relatively small number of products; this was accompanied by rapid concentration and the sifting out of undercapitalized and poorly managed small- and medium-sized firms. When experience did not confirm this strategy, the industry increasingly turned to production of specialty products, often on a small scale. This turn in strategy was accompanied by two developments. First, medium- and small-sized firms, whose flexibility was an asset for these tasks, came to the fore. Second, the rationalization of the production process, aimed at coping with rising wage costs, accelerated. Both processes were greatly helped by the proximity of efficient textile machinery and chemical industries. The productivity increases between 1970 and 1978 which resulted outpaced the manufacturing average. There were relatively small losses in total production capacity despite the continued closings of firms and sharp reductions in employment.

The West German banks often played an important role in this transformation. The relationship between the banks and the large companies appears unique in the sense that banks have high equity participation as well as loan commitments in the textile industry. As shareholders, they were highly committed to the survival of their companies and were ready to provide financial, managerial, and other support to their clients. In many instances, the banks initiated the reorganization and restructuring of troubled companies into smaller, flexible units.

In the clothing industry, adjustment to the changing economic environment was accomplished by specialization in high-quality goods. For instance, West Germany is currently the foremost exporter of ladies' outerwear and coats. Substitution of labor took place to a great extent in the form of offshore processing, especially subcontracting of low-priced clothing items to neighboring and especially to the Eastern and less developed European countries. Restricted to manufacturing firms only, the West German value-added duty system gave the clothing industry the opportunity to use profits earned on subcontracting to cross subsidize to a certain degree its high-cost domestically produced products, thus considerably improving its competitive position for these items.

Although the West German textile sector shows labor force characteristics similar to those of other countries, the social consequences of the dramatic labor adjustment process were attenuated by the fact that it started fairly early during a period of fast overall economic growth. Moreover, the relatively even distribution of the industry throughout the country, though there exist some important textile "pockets," allowed for the provision of alternative jobs for displaced labor. Finally, much of the reduction in employment took the form of attrition, which affected foreign workers.

An overview of the transformations that the West Germans have achieved in their textile and apparel industries can be gleaned from the statistics taken from OECD records and from industry sources. From

1964 to 1984, imports of textile and clothing goods rose from 4 billion DM to 31 billion DM. Exports increased at a similar pace in the same period, from 2.6 billion DM to 22.7 billion DM in 1984. Exports became such an important outlet for domestic production that by 1983, 45 percent of total production was exported, making West Germany, after Italy, the most important textile and clothing exporter in the world. However, owing to a higher starting point for imports, their absolute increase is higher than that of exports. In consequence, the import surplus grew to 8.7 billion DM in 1984, as compared to 1.4 billion DM twenty years ago. Measured in relation to sales, imports reached 17 percent in 1960. In 1983, this figure jumped to 56 percent. Thirty percent of these imports were from developing countries.

Growth in the textile and apparel trade deficit has quite naturally been accompanied by a loss of employment, which was further accelerated by industry restructuring. During the past twenty years, 350,000 jobs were lost in the textile sector alone. The work force thus decreased by nearly three-fifths, and representation of textile workers in the overall manufacturing labor force dropped from 5.4 percent in 1970 to 3.6 percent in 1983. Simultaneously, the number of enterprises in the textile industry was reduced from 3,100 to 1,400. Mergers were not the driving force behind this development, since, as we have noted, the West German textile industry is still characterized by small and medium-sized enterprises.

Production in the textile industry reached its peak in 1972. In the following years, apart from cyclical fluctuations, the level of production declined. By 1983, production was about one-fifth lower than in 1972. This decrease was, however, not nearly as dramatic as the corresponding reduction in employment and in the number of enterprises. The principal reason for production remaining relatively strong is that productivity increased by 85 percent between 1970 and 1983. What remains of the West German textile and apparel industries is, therefore, doing relatively well. Sales increased continually in the last two decades and reached a value of nearly 35 billion DM in textiles and 21 billion DM in clothing. This represents a growth of 5.8 percent a year in textiles and 6.3 percent in apparel. Investments were 1.2 billion DM in 1983, or 3.7 percent of sales. Investments have averaged around 1 billion DM for the past fifteen years.

One can conclude by saying that the West German textile and apparel industries have undergone an extensive restructuring in the last twenty years which was not accompanied by significant government assistance. Rather, it was helped by enlightened and cooperative trade unions, an economy capable of absorbing a large number of redundant textile and apparel workers, and assistance from the banks. Presently, it is a relatively small, decentralized industry, characterized by a high degree of specialization and high productivity.

Italy. In the 1970s, Italy emerged as the world's largest net exporter of textiles and clothing, steadily increasing its market share. The performance of the Italian industry compared favorably not only with other industrial countries but with most developing countries as well. This performance was the more impressive in the face of unusually high and rapidly growing labor costs in the larger textile mills. Of all OECD countries in our study, Italy alone has not experienced a decline in production.

In the years 1975–85, large, vertically integrated firms were replaced, wherever possible, by small firms specialized by products or production phases. Out of a total of 4,237 companies in the Italian textile industry in 1981, OECD figures show that 2,553, or 60 percent, employed between twenty and forty-nine persons and provided about 24 percent of all employment in the textile industry. This reorganization was primarily a reaction to the very rapid growth of labor costs in the early seventies and to the constraints on labor mobility and flexibility in large firms which were imposed by legislation and by the trade unions.

This change in the size of industry firms is more prevalent in certain sectors. The move to smaller establishments has been particularly noticeable in woolen fabrics, knitting, and clothing, those industries showing the best export performances. The smaller establishments have proven successful because in many textile productions and in clothing industry as well, economies of scale proved less relevant than financial and organizational economies. Consequently, the profitability of small firms is now higher than that of the large ones.

Furthermore, the "deverticalization" of the production cycle took advantage of the high geographical concentration of the textile industry in some small areas (such as Biella and Prato for the wool industry, Como for the silk industry), where the costs of transportation between firms is low and where the exchange of information is easily accomplished. In the clothing and knitting industries, the adjustment process was accompanied by a growing recourse to independent workers and was aimed at achieving an increasing specialization by product. The rapidly changing pattern of demand offered many small enterprises the opportunity to enter segments of the market, particularly casual and sports clothes, with new, high-quality products.

The smaller firms also benefited from lower labor costs, according to the firm size, location, and the different legal regulations applying to independent workers. Several factors contribute to this situation. First, firms employing fewer than fifty workers legally escape the payment of a considerable part of the heavy employers' contribution. Second, the substantial development of outworking permits illegal avoidance of this contribution (the so-called underground labor phenomenon). Third, small firms that employ primarily family labor do not necessarily remunerate the work of family members, as would be done in an establishment employing wage labor. Fourth, the gradual shift of several branches of textiles and apparel from the northwest to the less unionized northeast and central Italy and to the southern region—probably affecting knitting and clothing more than the rest of textiles—reflects a move toward local labor markets with higher rates of open unemployment, hence greater possibilities for employing outworkers at low wages.

Finally, EEC import regulations have played an important role in the shift to smaller establishments, as they have provided sheltered outlets for efficient Italian producers. Indeed, Italian market shares increased more in the EEC than in other OECD markets. The depreciation of the lire also contributed to the Italian export performance, although to the extent that imported inputs were used, this has been partially mitigated.

Because of the use of equipment already in place, the shift to smaller production lines required relatively little additional fixed investment, and the companies could invest the funds saved in current assets such as receivables and inventories required in larger amounts by the new industrial structure. Their success has allowed small firms to improve their efficiency by adopting, when appropriate, the best available technology (mainly special-purpose machines) and more modern management techniques, such as computerized order and inventory control, thus reinforcing their position further.

On the other hand, large textile and apparel groups have not performed well. While they have not necessarily disappeared, they have been either nationalized or are more flexibly organized and connected with a number of small, independent firms through financial (and sometimes marketing) linkages. Government intervention has been aimed at maintaining (or at least slowing the decline of) employment in the large textile companies and in the traditional textile area through subsidies and other forms of financial assistance. But, given constraints on laying off labor, many of these firms could not adopt adequate conversion plans. They were taken over by public holdings—which now account for about 5 percent of total employment in textiles and more than 10 percent in clothing, with large production shares in some lines such as cotton yarn, men's suits, and ladies' outerwear—and continue to depend on public financial support. Many large, privately owned enterprises benefited from other public interventions, such as the cheap loans offered under the Textile Act, and almost all the textile and clothing companies took advantage of both the partial budgetization of the social changes introduced after 1975 to help industries that are in difficulty and the system of compensating short-term workers. But Italy's solid export performance is mainly attributable to the work of the smaller private enterprises, with little outside support.

A consequence of Italy's free-form adjustment process has been weakness in research and development activities, notably in manmade fibers, and a failure to modernize the highly capital-intensive parts of the industry. Moreover, the neglect of working conditions by some smaller firms and of environmental conditions by the larger groups in the textile industry will require costly corrective action.

The Italian industry is now an aggressive, international competitor in specialized quality synthetics and high-fashion design. It is supported by highly specialized, small, yet vertically cooperative production units that benefit from an ability to remain flexible, to make product changes quickly, and to upgrade technology.

United Kingdom. As the oldest textile manufacturer, the United Kingdom had already been confronted with major adjustment problems during the interwar period. After World War II, its difficulties were compounded by the emergence of substantial excess capacity. This excess was caused by dissipating overseas markets, increasing imports from Commonwealth countries, and the failure of the industry to rationalize. The situation stimulated what has proven to be a long history of government intervention aimed at reducing excess capacity, increasing productivity, and recently, under the impact of the recession, securing employment. Continuously supported by government policies designed to protect the domestic market against increasing pressure from imports, the series of government measures, starting with the Cotton Act in 1959, attempted with varying success to provide the industry with long-term stability. Though these measures achieved some improvement in productivity and efficiency, many segments of the textile and clothing industries achieved insufficient rationalization to forego continued direct and indirect protection. The textile industry experienced moderate expansion up to 1973 as the result of a very strong performance in knitting, and a steady decline in output until 1979, when it shrank abruptly by 25 percent in that year alone.

Originally highly fragmented and composed of a large number of small firms that were production- rather than market-oriented, the industry's structure was influenced by the government's policy of encouraging mergers to produce units of more efficient dimensions. The most sustained impact on the structure of the industry, however, came from the acquisition activities pursued successively by the two important manmade fiber producers in the early 1960s, Courtaulds and ICI. Courtaulds' strategy can best be described as an attempt to guarantee outlets for its fiber production through the mass manufacture of yarns and fabrics, especially cotton and manmade fiber fabrics, and to displace low-cost Commonwealth suppliers who had been gaining an increasing share of the cotton textile markets. It was believed that the economies of scale and market power achieved as a result of consolidation and modernization would reduce costs sufficiently to make domestically produced textiles competitive with imports. This strategy was predicated on a domestic market protected against low-cost competition. ICI, the largest UK fiber producer, reacted to Courtaulds' actions by financing (but not managing) the growth of alternative large textile groups. Many of these large groups integrated forward into apparel and developed significant foreign investments, many of these in the Commonwealth.

By 1973, it became apparent that this overall strategy had not been successful. In particular, the mass market approach led to product developments inadequate to meet changing conditions. It tended to divert attention away from specialization, from developing new outlets, and from marketing. In several clothing lines, poor marketing and fashion performance resulted in the loss of highly profitable markets, both abroad and—after the United Kingdom's accession to the European Community—at home. Moreover, the textile (and synthetic fiber) industry's bias toward hardware and production resulted in persistent excess capacity combined with low profitability. A last important feature, which was both cause and consequence of the difficulties of the United Kingdom textile sector, was the decline of the textile-machinery industry, which gradually lost ground on the domestic market and suffered from an abrupt fall in its market share abroad. While in some areas close association with large manmade fiber producers led UK companies to innovate and become world leaders, the overall technological performance has been rather poor. Between 1976 and 1982, for instance, investment in shuttleless looms was lower than Spain's.

Currently, UK productivity remains low, slightly half that of the United States. Production and employment are down as well. In 1981, output in carpets ran at two-thirds of 1977 levels, and employment in manmade fiber production fell from 29,800 in December 1978 to 12,700 in December 1981, a decrease of over 60 percent. At the same time, imports have risen sharply. In just the two-year period between 1980 and 1982, employment in the textile industry dropped from 346.6 thousand workers to 280.4 thousand (a 19 percent decline), while employment in the apparel industry dropped from 257.2 thousand to 204.9 thousand (a decrease of 20 percent). Whereas the British textile industry was once characterized by medium-scale (50–500 worker) firms, it is now dominated by a few very large firms. The recession-induced partial collapse of UK textile production since 1979 has accelerated the trend toward concentration.

The outlook is not entirely gloomy, however. In 1983, Vantona-Viyella, formed from Vantona Textiles and Carrington Viyella, invested £25 million on high-tech plants and machinery. Earnings climbed from the break-even point to £25 million in 1984. Furthermore, the government has recently embarked on a four-year plan to aid small- and medium-sized companies in the textile, clothing, and footwear sectors to invest in technologically advanced equipment. This initiative has been welcomed by the industry, with the reservation that the sums allocated for the program are far too small in relation to the massive aid extended to other sectors, notably steel and mining, and in relation to the aid packages of some other Western European countries, such as Belgium and France.

France. The changes in the French textile and apparel industries have been extremely complex. In the wake of rapid economic expansion in the 1950s, considerable modernization and concentration took place. A major trend encouraged by government incentives was the mass market approach, especially in yarn and cloth production. The goal was to try to reduce labor costs and increase specialization. This strategy seemed to work, despite the gradual loss of sheltered markets overseas and the relaxation of protection, notably within the EEC, because the domestic market was growing rapidly. Certain lines emerged as leaders. Knitting, luxury children's wear, and underwear all performed strongly.

In the early 1970s, however, demand slowed and market segments entered a period of stagnation or decline. These changed economic conditions found most of the French textile industry overextended and undercapitalized. France met the crisis in textiles by adopting protectionist measures and encouraging further mergers designed to produce firms that would be capable of sustaining the costs involved in upgrading technology. Although the government provided transitional assistance to small- and medium-sized firms, consolidation was not even then accomplished evenly. A great deal of the industry remained fragmented and antiquated, while a few large and powerful groups emerged. Concentration of the industry reached the point in 1975 where the top three firms accounted for 30 percent of all spindles and looms installed. By 1982, 40 percent of all persons working in the textile industry in France worked in companies having five hundred employees or more.

These firms differ from the large textile firms in other EC countries in that they are often conglomerates rather than the traditional, vertically integrated units. They often lack the flexibility to keep abreast of market conditions. Although the French government has encouraged extensive technological research to raise productivity, it has risen no faster than anywhere else. And these measures did nothing to halt the steady and substantial decline in registered employment which occurred as many of these firms were encountering serious difficulties. In fact, the emphasis on productivity rather than marketing seems to have accelerated declines in the labor levels.

Despite these setbacks, the French continue to subsidize the industry. Under the Mitterrand government, the policy of aid for the textile industry includes the following: investment/employment measures, known as "contracts of solidarity"; a 12 percent reduction in social charges; preferential rate loans; and the establishment of a textile promotion center. In 1982–83, the French government, in the form of the Arnoux Commission, initiated a formal policy study to identify industrial sectors that would benefit from preferential public support. The inclusion of textiles along with such industries as aerospace stems primarily from political considerations, not market realities. The success of a publicly driven strategy for textiles and apparel remains to be seen.

The Case of Japan

Much has been written about the performance of the Japanese economy since the end of World War II, and it is unnecessary here to rehearse observations that are common knowledge. It should suffice, then, to review briefly the salient points that differentiate the Japanese economic system from the economic systems of its major OECD competitors.

The Department of Commerce reports that as of April 1985, industrial production in Japan had reached 273.6, using 1967 as a base level. No other country in the OECD came close to achieving such growth. Investment as a percentage of GDP was the highest in the OECD; hourly earnings for production workers in manufacturing increased at the highest rate; and its share of world trade was second only to that of the United States. Japan has maintained strong growth in the 1980s, while the European economies have faltered. Between 1981 and second quarter 1984, Japan's real GNP climbed 11 percent.

It has been pointed out often that an important characteristic of the Japanese system—one which sets it apart from many OECD countries— is public and private emphasis on maximizing net exports. Another significant difference between Japan and the other industrialized nations is that there is very little intrasectoral trade in Japan's key export sectors, as distinguished from other OECD nations, whose trade is predominantly intrasectoral. Japan exports in these sectors but has almost no imports in return. Consequently, import penetration into the Japanese market has been kept to a minimum. Between 1970 and 1983, while the import share of the U.S. domestic market more than doubled, from 8 percent to a little under 19 percent, and while the share of the EC internal market for manufactures claimed by suppliers outside the Community rose from 11 to 17 percent, the level of imports in Japan increased only from 6.4 percent to 8.6 percent. Nonetheless, despite the policies that have produced the enviable growth which characterizes the Japanese manufacturing sector, the Japanese textile and apparel industries have experienced difficulties similar to those which have afflicted Japan's European and American counterparts.

The textile and apparel industries played a crucial role in the initial phases of Japan's industrial development. In the early 1950s, Japan was virtually the only exporter of textile products in the Far East. During the 1970s, however, voluntary restraints that had been placed on exports to the United States, along with the import restrictions imposed by European governments, which were a factor in Japanese trade in the 1950s and 1960s, lost much of their meaning as Japan's competitive position in these markets was extensively eroded by wage increases and currency appreciation. Decline in the domestic industry was further augmented by measures encouraging overseas investment. Investments in Asian nations started in the 1960s and accelerated in the early 1970s. These measures were undertaken in part to combat the problem of import limitations imposed by foreign governments. Big spinning companies (as well as synthetic fiber producers) relocated part of their activities in developing countries. Japanese involvement in the Asian NICs' textile industries is easily underestimated. Japan's joint ventures still control most of the synthetic-fiber sector in this region. Another factor in the decline of the Japanese domestic textile industry was that most firms hesitated to scrap and to rebuild fast enough. They had large investments tied up in machinery for the production of cotton, woolen, and rayon fabrics and did not resolutely switch to the new synthetic fibers.

During the same period, the industry faced growing competition from Asian countries for Asian markets, for the lucrative U.S. market, and for the Japanese domestic market. At the same time, the import of textile goods increased dramatically. The market share of imports (imports divided by domestic demand) climbed rapidly upward, from 0.5 percent in 1960 to 18.3 percent in 1978. As a result, Japan's trade balance of textile goods deteriorated quickly, and the trade balance, including textile raw materials, dropped into the red in 1979.

The decline of the Japanese textile and apparel industries can be gauged from statistics indicating the relative weight of the textile industry in Japan's economy. In 1950, 23.7 percent of total shipments of manufacturing industries and 48.2 percent of total exports were textiles. In 1970, these figures had dropped to 7.7 percent and 12.5 percent, respectively, and by 1980 they had fallen to 5.2 percent and 4.8 percent. The continuing business slump also took a heavy toll on textile jobs: in the eight-year period 1970–79, the number of textile workers decreased by approximately 320,000 (18 percent). The textile industry's share of those employed in manufacturing fell from 23 percent in 1955 to 13.4 percent in 1979. In 1977, a total of 1,328 textile firms (manufacturers as well as marketing companies) went bankrupt, and outstanding debts amounted to an all-time high of $1.3 billion. The number of business failures in the following years remained at a high level, reaching 1,388 for 1979.

The Japanese response to these developments is in the tradition of a series of measures enacted by the government since the mid-1950s. The thrust of the initial efforts was retooling, with the idea of bringing export capacity in line with the country's trade possibilities; since 1974, as part of Japan's overall industrial orientation toward knowledge-intensive industries, the emphasis changed to research and development in the production of high-value-added products; to the promotion of vertical integration between weaving, clothing, and other activities; and to the development of a modern, quality-oriented clothing industry. The Japanese industry also undertook strategies designed to provide it with regional superiority in technology and production of synthetic-blended fabrics and apparel. These strategies have been successful. As their expertise increased, the Japanese transferred more mature and tested technology to less developed Asian countries to upgrade their FDI (foreign direct investment) and maintain their international competitiveness in other countries.

In 1979, Japan enacted a law for "structural improvement to the textile industry" to further these ends. To aid the Japanese textile industry in regaining its vigor and stability, the government decided that the industry must successfully meet the following challenges:

1. It had to work out a viable strategy to cope with the growing competition from neighboring developing countries in ways that are compatible with the ideal of the international division of labor.

2. It had to find ways to meet the increasingly diversified preferences of domestic consumers.

3. It had to restructure itself to create an industry capable of offering

employment opportunities that appeal to the changing values of workers.

In order to meet these goals, Japanese textile manufacturers worked closely with apparel makers and embarked on joint research projects and product development activities with them. There are several very large fiber makers and spinners that have achieved good vertical distribution. For instance, Toray Industries, one of Japan's larger fiber companies, wholly or partly owns numerous fabric and apparel companies in Japan and in other nations in Asia. Textile and fiber companies have also switched over to nontextile businesses, such as cosmetics, polyester film, carbon fiber, interferon, reverse osmosis membranes, and even housing construction. This shift makes them less vulnerable to reverses in the textile market. Nonfiber product sales amounted to 71 percent of sales for Asahi Chemical Company (the largest textile company in Japan), 36 percent of sales for Toray (the second largest), 27 percent for Teijin (the third largest). The government contributed to this process by releasing funds from government-run financial institutions to help industry switch to more promising business areas.

Most firms in the Japanese textile and apparel complex, however, are extremely small. In the apparel industry, the average number of workers per plant in 1977 was 12.6, while only 1.3 percent of apparel plants employed more than 1,000 workers. A similar situation exists in the textile industry. Most plants employ fewer than 20 workers. The abundance of these small firms provides the advantage of encouraging the accumulation of skills and know-how in small, highly specialized units capable of adjusting to changes in textile materials and products lines according to the needs of export markets. These small textile mills work most efficiently when associated with larger firms. About half of the small firms are linked with large synthetic fiber producers. These producers install the small textile companies' facilities, determine their product lines, and guide their sales operations. The other 40 to 50 percent of capacity is in the hands of independent mills, and it is these mills in particular that tend to have poor production facilities. Most of these firms are tiny family mills that are not capable of adjustment, because their owners, living in relatively isolated areas, cannot easily change occupations. Therefore, the Japanese government has encouraged them to develop closer ties with larger companies. Under the Law on Extraordinary Measures for the Structural Improvement of Textile Industries enacted in July 1979, the government provided tax and financial incentives to smaller firms that undertook projects within the guidelines laid out by the Ministry of International Trade and Industry (MITI) to encourage vertical cooperation.

During the years after these measures were enacted, the apparel industry, which had been performing relatively strongly since World War II, turned sluggish as the domestic market became saturated. This development was taken into account when these programs were renewed in 1984. At that time, Japan's Textile Industry Council and the Textile Industry Committee of the Industrial Structure Council identified several factors that had led to the deterioration of the industry:

1. declining demand for textile products, owing to the general slowdown of economic growth and maturity of the textile and apparel market

2. rising production costs, because of the necessity of producing a large variety of products in small lots to meet the diversification of consumer tastes and demands

3. gains by Korean and U.S. producers as a result of rationalization and upgrading of production facilities

The Textile Industry Council and the Textile Industry Committee urged further restructuring efforts, including scrapping outmoded or unused machinery, that were designed to improve concentration on the development of differentiated, high-value-added production. They set as goals the development of small-batch, wide-variety manufacturing technology, partially subsidized by MITI. Apparel makers were encouraged to concentrate on limiting their production to the quantity they were certain to sell; to reconsider the wisdom of mass-production strategies; and to increase efficiency. MITI has also proposed the creation of a Fashion Community Center to further these efforts.

The process of restructuring is ongoing. For instance, on March 19, 1985, the *Japanese Economic Journal* reported that five textile trade organizations had decided to scrap excessive machinery to counter a recession and rising imports from developing countries. This program, once it had been approved by MITI, was to be enacted over a three-year period and would involve a total of 8,561 textile makers and another 353 yarn-twisting firms.

These adjustment efforts and policies have been successful in promoting the restructuring and modernization of Japan's textile and apparel industries. It can be said that these industries have had to face in about thirty years a succession of adjustment problems which in some older industrial countries stretched over a century or more. Adjustment was helped initially by the sustained expansion of domestic demand, but as the increase in domestic consumption slowed, the Japanese have proven themselves relatively adept at making the sudden shifts in strategy needed to meet the changes in external supply-and-demand conditions which have characterized the industry in the past twenty years—conditions which were aggravated by sharp fluctuations in the exchange rate and in feed-stock prices. On the whole, the record appears to be quite impressive. This model of controlled, publicly supported, and gradual adjustment generally seems to have been effective in restructuring the industry, so that it now has a more solid base.

Assessment of the Performance of the Textile and Apparel Industries in Major OECD Countries

During the 1950s and 1960s, the textile and apparel industries of the OECD countries referred to in our study enjoyed the prosperity created by the reconstruction that followed World War II. Consumption rose steadily throughout the period, particularly in former Axis countries whose economies had been almost totally destroyed by the war. Japan was also able to benefit from its position in relation to Asian markets, and its relatively low production costs in the labor-intensive textile and apparel industries stimulated the growth of its exports to the other OECD countries, particularly the United States.

During the late 1960s and early 1970s, conditions began to change. The domestic markets ceased growing at significant rates. The United Kingdom and France—both countries that were still major colonial powers after the war and that maintained close contacts with former colonies after the colonies had been granted their independence—began to experience a flood of low-cost imports from these countries. And the NICs began to emerge in Asia, severely cutting Japanese textile exports by virtue of their lower labor costs. The initial response of the OECD countries was to emphasize increased production and mass marketing. They hoped that economies of scale would enable them to maintain their competitiveness. This strategy proved unsuccessful because it led to the formation of large, rather inflexible firms that were unable to respond to the rapidly changing market and fashion conditions that began to characterize the industry. Furthermore, the economies of scale that emerged did not offset the lower labor costs that developing-nation exporters enjoyed.

The United Kingdom and France still have textile and apparel industries that are highly concentrated. Despite efforts to maintain employment in these segments, they have shrunk dramatically during the last ten years and have become increasingly uncompetitive.

The Germans and the Japanese have fared much better. They both now have relatively small though highly efficient textile industries that produce specialized products. The apparel industries of both these countries emphasize sophisticated, high-fashion garments, and in recent years Tokyo has become one of the design centers of the world. Germany and Japan accomplished these ends in different ways. The Germans provided little government support for restructuring and let market forces control adjustment. These circumstances have encouraged the formation of small- and medium-sized firms capable of responding to changes in market conditions quickly and effectively. The emphasis on smaller firms is congenial to the German industry, which has a tradition of small, family-owned enterprises. The German government has, however, promoted adjustment in the apparel industry by encouraging offshore production. The Japanese government, on the other had, has taken a much more active role in the restructuring of both the apparel and the textile industries. It passed a series of measures designed to encourage increased cooperation between various downstream and upstream components of the industry and provided incentives to scrap outmoded or underutilized machinery in an effort to reduce capacity. It has also assisted the apparel industry in shifting to high-fashion garments.

The end result of the restructuring process in these four OECD countries—West Germany, Italy, the United Kingdom, and France—is that the textile and apparel industries have shrunken by at least 50 percent in employment during the last twenty years, and their importance in the overall economic performance of these countries has declined. Only Italy has maintained textile and apparel industries that are both vital and growing. It is difficult to tell, however, whether government measures designed to promote adjustment of the industries are responsible for their success or whether the success is the product of Italian entrepreneurial instincts. By and large, the textile and apparel industries are composed of thousands of small firms that display a high degree of cooperation with one another and are therefore capable of quick response to changes in the marketplace. Those larger firms which still exist—they employ less than one-tenth of the work force—have been taken over by the government and are essentially moribund. As a result of these changes, the Italians have emerged as the preeminent exporter of textiles and apparel.

4

The U.S. Response to Increased International Competition: The Case of the Textile and Apparel Industries

The response of the United States to changes in the international market for textiles and apparel has been less programmatic than the responses of its OECD counterparts. Government involvement has centered on trade measures such as tariffs and quantitative restrictions. Although the problems that currently beset the American textile and apparel complex should not be underestimated, these industries have done relatively well when compared to their OECD counterparts. Germany and Japan have dismantled vast segments of their industries, and the French and British industries are stagnating. Only in Italy have the textile and apparel industries made a strong showing, and even there the dismal showing of the large, state-owned complexes detracts somewhat from the excellent performance turned in by the small, local establishments. The U.S. textile industry has performed strongly in comparison to the industries of Europe and Japan. Although the U.S. apparel industry has not done as well, it certainly has done no worse than the apparel industries of most of our industrialized counterparts.

The United States has retained a considerable advantage in labor productivity levels over the OECD countries covered in this book. This reflects the technological advantage gained by new equipment as well as the superior efficiency with which labor is deployed. The United States has performed especially well in textiles, where the nature of the market allows for greater specialization. In spinning and weaving, unit labor costs in Europe were significantly higher than they were in the United States. This is so despite the fact that hourly labor costs in the United States in the textile industry were higher than in the other nations addressed in this book. Low unit-labor costs can be attributed, therefore, to vastly higher worker productivity. In fact, the United States had the highest level of productivity of all major international producers. The U.S. advantage in unit-labor costs promises to grow if the dollar returns to levels indicated by recent trade performance. Furthermore, supplementary labor costs are now lower in the United States than in many other countries. Between 1970 and 1980, the rate of increase in hourly labor costs for the U.S. manufacturing sector, including the textile and apparel industries, was one of the world's lowest. In other words, during this period, hourly labor costs in the United States were declining relative to those of other OECD countries. In addition, the United States has not been as heavily hit as other OECD nations by losses in employment, nor has it found it as difficult to recruit and retain labor.

In this chapter, we will examine the elements that constitute the U.S. response to the onslaught of imports from the NICs and other developing countries. We will review the measures taken by the government to stem the flood of imports, as well as critiques that have been offered of these policies. We will also consider the steps taken by the textile, apparel, and retailing industries to meet this challenge, a challenge intensified by the declining rates of U.S. consumption and the overvaluation of the dollar.

Official U.S. Trade Policy

The Arrangement Regarding International Trade in Textiles (known as the Multifiber Arrangement, or MFA) is currently the framework designed to provide orderly trade in textiles and apparel. The MFA should be seen as an outgrowth of efforts that began in the mid-1950s to regulate the worldwide trade of textiles and apparel. At that time, the U.S. industry was faced with increased imports of Japanese cotton textiles and apparel. These products were chiefly low-value-added, low-cost fabrics and women's and children's apparel. Increased imports from Japan, coupled with the growth of the textile industry in Latin America—formerly a market for U.S. exports—led the industry to seek relief through the imposition of restrictions on imports.

Negotiations were begun under the auspices of the General Agreement on Tariffs and Trade (GATT). As a result, the United States and Japan signed a reciprocal trade agreement in 1957 which gave tariff concessions to the Japanese on certain products. Under the Trade Agreements Act, the U.S. Tariff Commission had the responsibility of determining whether the trade agreement concessions they granted led to imports that posed a threat of injury or market disruption to the U.S. market. In the event of market disruption, the commission could apply tariff relief (in the form of surcharges) for the domestic industry, thus negating the previously negotiated concessions. The Japanese, in turn, implemented a plan to reduce cotton textile exports voluntarily for five years. Italy also agreed to limit its exports of certain cotton goods.

The weakness of these bilateral arrangements became apparent almost immediately. Hong Kong and certain countries began increasing their exports to the United States dramatically. By 1960, this rapid growth allowed Hong Kong to replace Japan as the single largest textile exporter to the United States, a fact that led the Japanese to reexamine their own determination to adhere to voluntary quotas.

The increase of imports from so many different countries underscored the need for a uniform method of dealing with this problem. In November 1959, steps were taken under GATT to initiate talks regarding a multilateral approach toward limiting the growth of textile imports to developed countries. The meetings eventually produced consensus on a list of some of the elements of market disruption. The contracting parties to GATT also agreed to seek constructive solutions to claims of market injury through consultations between the parties involved. A permanent GATT body, the Committee on Avoidance of Market Disruptions, was created to facilitate this process.

Nonetheless, imports of textile products continued to grow in the early 1960s. President John F. Kennedy announced the creation of a new cabinet committee (chaired by the secretary of commerce) to study the problems facing domestic textile and apparel producers. The committee was to "explore such questions as the competitive position of the U.S. textile industry and its ability to meet the pressure of imports."

In May 1961 the president introduced a seven-point program based on the findings of the cabinet committee. This program led to the creation in July 1961 of the Short-Term Arrangement Regarding International Trade in Cotton Textiles (STA), the first international agreement regarding the trade of cotton textiles. The STA covered sixty-four categories of cotton products. It specified the conditions of market disruption and spelled out the procedures by which an importing country could respond to such conditions. Once market disruption was established, the supplying country had thirty days to limit its exports to the base level (July 1960 through June 1961). If it failed to curb exports during this period, the importing country had the right to restrict imports to that level. Consultation was encouraged during the thirty-day period, however, and category provisions were flexible. The STA provided a model for all subsequent international textile arrangements.

The Long Term Cotton Arrangement (LTA) was signed by representatives of nineteen governments on February 9, 1962. It was renewed twice, in 1967 and 1970, and remained in effect until 1973. By that time, it had been signed by thirty-three countries. It doubled the consultation period to sixty days and defined the base level as a twelve-month period ending three months prior to the request for restraint. If no agreement was reached, the LTA required that after a year the restraint levels be raised by 5 percent, the approximate growth of the U.S. market at that time. It also established guidelines for bilateral agreements.

As a result of the LTA, new suppliers were given generous quotas, and the larger suppliers were restricted from growing too quickly. The number of countries included under this agreement testifies to the growing international trade. The problems that developed from this arrangement reflect changes in the mix of products these countries were capable of producing. During this period, developing nations, particularly the large Asian suppliers, began to switch to the production of manmade fiber and textiles. These articles, along with woolens, were not controlled under the LTA, which put new pressure on the U.S. textile and apparel industries. In 1960, imports of manmade fiber textiles totaled 31 million pounds, but by 1970, this figure had grown to 329 million pounds.

In 1971, the United States negotiated bilateral agreements covering wool and manmade fiber goods with Hong Kong, Japan, Korea, and Taiwan. It also conducted similar negotiations with Malaysia. These agreements set the stage for a more inclusive arrangement. In 1974, fifty countries joined in negotiating and signing the Multifiber Arrangement. The MFA was originally negotiated to cover the period from January 1, 1974 through December 31, 1977. It has been renewed three times and currently is in force through July 31, 1991. Among its principal features is that it extended coverage to include manmade fibers and wool textiles and clothing. It also made provision for a Textile Surveillance Body to collect data that could serve as a basis for quantitative restrictions. Article 3 of the MFA authorizes the imposition of unilateral restraints against imports that disrupt or threaten to disrupt home-country markets. The base period used in evaluating disruptions was defined as the twelve-month period that began two months before the consultation call, and the growth rate on restraints was set at 6 percent annually.

The principal purpose of the MFA, however, is to serve as an umbrella under which signatory countries negotiate bilateral agreements. It specifies that in bilateral agreements, growth rates and bases should be more liberal than under the MFA itself. Currently, U.S. bilateral agreements vary widely in their ability to control growth of imports from individual countries. Only a small number of products are subject to specific restraints, and consultation does not usually occur until after import surges have disrupted the U.S. market.

Bilateral agreements are generally negotiated under Article 4 of the MFA. The agreements with Taiwan and other nonsignatories to the MFA, while not under Article 4, nonetheless follow the framework set out in the MFA. The agreements with the three major suppliers to the United States—Taiwan, Hong Kong, and South Korea—are more restrictive than those with other suppliers. This was accomplished by invoking the provision of paragraph 6 of the Protocol of Understanding to the MFA negotiated in 1981, which states that the major supplying countries can be treated more restrictively than other countries.

One weakness for the United States of the original MFA, as we have noted, was that it allowed for a minimum annual growth rate of 6 percent in imports. However, because the U.S. market never reached this level of growth, imports came to take over a progressively greater share of the market. In later revisions of the MFA, "reasonable departures" from this growth rate were permitted.

In the United States, responsibility for the administration and implementation of textile and apparel agreements resides in two interagency bodies. Overall policy decisions are made by the Textile Trade Policy Group. The administration of trade agreements is left to the Committee for the Implementation of Textile Agreements (CITA). It is CITA's responsibility to determine when and if market disruption has occurred and to request consultation with the government involved. Negotiations are then carried out under the leadership of the chief textile negotiator in the Office of the U.S. Trade Representative. Day-to-day monitoring of imports affected by bilateral agreements is conducted by the Department of Commerce's Office of Textiles and Apparel (OTEXA) under the direction of CITA.

OTEXA tracks the levels of imports from each country. Weekly reviews are held to determine whether a market disruption has occurred or is threatening to occur. Although the chairman of CITA is granted by law the right to request a consultation as long as a majority of CITA board members do not object, in practice the decision is made by consensus. Factors usually considered are domestic production, market share, volume of imports, and the import production ratio.

Input from the private sector is provided through a variety of channels. The American Fiber Textile and Apparel Coalition meets regularly with CITA and includes representatives from the American Textile Manufacturers Institute, the American Apparel Manufacturers Association, the Man-Made Fiber Producers Association, the Amalgamated Clothing and Textile Workers Union, the International Ladies Garment Workers Union, and other organizations representing various segments of the complex.

The MFA has been subject to much criticism from within the textile and apparel industries and from without. No other U.S. industry has been the subject of an agreement like the MFA, and critics have maintained that it violates the principle of free trade. Furthermore, they point out that such an agreement has costs that must be absorbed by consumers and by the U.S. economy. Michael C. Munger of the Center for the Study of American Business at Washington University estimated that quantitative restrictions on apparel and textiles cost the U.S. consumer $3.4 billion (measured in 1980 dollars) in 1982, in addition to tariffs on textiles and apparel in 1980, which cost $16.8 billion. He concluded that "in many instances, consumers would be better off if they could somehow pay the worker his or her present salary (with fringe benefits) *to do nothing,* and allow free import of the restricted product." In a study on the effect of quantitative restrictions on textile imports from Hong Kong on the U.S. economy, Morris E. Morkre of the Federal Trade Commission concluded that for the year 1980, the costs to the U.S. economy was $308 million. The major share of this is an economic rent created by the quotas, which represents a transfer of real income from the United States to Hong Kong. Morkre further concluded that the beneficial effects of quotas on U.S. employment in the textile and apparel industries was small. He suggested that if the quotas were removed, employment would drop by only 8,900 workers, which would involve unemployment costs of $17 million.

Other critics, most notably from the textile and apparel industries, point out that the MFA has at best merely reduced the effect of imports on the U.S. textile and apparel industries; it has hardly stemmed the tide of imports, and the alleged costs created for the consumer have been exaggerated. Their objections to reports that detail these costs center on three areas:

1. the assumption that the rent on quotas is passed on in its entirety to the consumer
2. the belief that in the absence of quotas or tariffs, prices would actually drop
3. the idea that the number of jobs preserved by existing arrangements is inconsequential

Industry leaders believe that the level of imports has reached crisis proportions despite the MFA. Thomas Roboz of the Stanwood Corporation has called the flood of imports "an unmitigated disaster," and Eugene C. Gwaltney of the Russel Corporation squarely placed the blame for this situation on the MFA. He noted in *Textile World*, "There are so many holes in MFA, the thing is going to collapse. The way it's been chopped up and added to, it's impossible to police the program. I think it should be revised in its entirety." Industry leaders cite a recent study by Data Resources which concluded that 2 million jobs in textile, apparel, and related industries will be lost in the next five years if the current rate of import growth is maintained. Data Resources also found that the current rate of import growth would result in a $21 billion trade deficit by 1990 and would contribute $24 billion to the federal deficit.

Ron Levin, head of OTEXA, admits that there have been serious problems with the bilaterals, but he believes that they "have in many ways been improved." He was quoted in *Textile World* as saying, "These are negotiations. They require give and take. You make your judgment on the overall package. In our efforts to negotiate improvements, some of the concessions may not have been worth some of the gains. Overall, we've had some pretty good negotiations." Other supporters, both in and out of government circles, point out that, though admittedly imperfect, the MFA is a significant achievement in that it reflects large-scale negotiations among parties of sharply conflicting interests to arrive at a system which, though it has not contained the flow of imports to the older industrial economies, has at least provided a modicum of stability and moderation.

The most glaring deficiencies of the bilateral agreements worked out under the MFA are not a function of the MFA itself but are the product of conditions that American negotiators have accepted in working out these agreements. Most bilateral agreements do not subject the majority of product categories to specific import restraints, and recently there has been a trend toward eliminating aggregate import ceilings in return for restrictions on specific products. Countries are often allowed to shift exports from a restrained product category to another. Relaxation of restraints progresses whether the importing country reaches them or not, thereby providing the importing country with considerable leeway for growth. Given these conditions, it is not surprising that agreements negotiated under the MFA have not halted the flow of imports into the United States.

Furthermore, critics such as the American Textile Manufacturers Institute maintain that existing programs have not been used aggressively. However, a recent General Accounting Office (GAO) report that reviewed the administration of the MFA found that CITA's decision-making process was generally adequate, although weighted toward protecting the domestic industry. The GAO's major criticisms were that it felt that market disruption statements could be better supported and more persuasive and that input from interested parties could be further facilitated.

The textile industry has fared much better than has the apparel industry under the MFA. It has produced sufficient stability to encourage the significant investment that has characterized the textile industry in the 1970s and 1980s. Resulting gains in productivity, augmented by the lower dollar value, contributed to the textile trade surplus of the latter 1970s. In sum, under the MFA, the textile industry was given time to revitalize itself, and, until the recent appreciation of the dollar, it performed strongly. The apparel industry, however, did not benefit as much from the MFA. While import controls have slowed the rate of increase in the number of units shipped, their value has increased sharply because of trading up in price points. Since all controls are on units, a major shift occurred in the mid-1970s toward higher-unit-priced garments, particularly from the Far East. Although slowing somewhat, this trend is still prevalent. Consequently, the trade deficit that the U.S. apparel industry had experienced since the 1950s steadily increased under the MFA. This in turn has affected the textile industry, which, as the domestic industry has declined, has faced a declining demand for fiber and yarn.

Item 807 of the Tariff Schedules

Some U.S. offshore manufacturing is done under this item, which permits U.S. manufacturers to export U.S. component parts and material for additional work and to pay duty only on the value added upon reentry into the United States. This includes sewing labor, overhead, and a fair profit for the contractor. A firm using 807 can own the offshore facility, use contractors, be engaged in a joint venture offshore, or work with organizations that provide packages. There are, however, several conditions that must be met. The exported parts and material must be ready for assembly without further fabrication; they must not lose their physical identity in the process; and they must not be advanced in value or improved in condition except by being assembled. These conditions ensure the utilization of domestic apparel skills in preparing material for shipments offshore. An 807 operation requires that the fabric be spread, cut, and assembled in the correct parts for sewing. Furthermore, the garments need to be finished and packaged after they are reimported.

In 1983, approximately 8 percent of the total square yardage of apparel imported was 807 apparel, down a point from 1982. This shift reflected a sharp rise in all imports, though, not a decrease in 807 imports. In 1983, 807 exports amounted to $350 million, a 41 percent increase over the 1978 level of $248 million. Mexico, with twin plant concepts in El Paso and other Texas areas and in southern California, is the most important 807 source. The other major countries are the Dominican Republic, Costa Rica, Haiti, Colombia, Honduras, Jamaica, Barbados, Guyana, and Panama.

The risks found in 807 operations are those associated with imports from most developing countries. It is difficult to control quality in an offshore 807 facility unless it is owned by the manufacturer. The sewing skills in many 807 countries may not be as good as those of U.S. operators, and certain garment types cannot be produced without considerable investment in training. Another problem is the lack of adequate technical personnel for supervision, machine repair, and quality inspection. A further disadvantage is that working capital for fabric, trim, and cutting labor is tied up longer when compared to domestic production. Most manufacturers have found this extra time to involve three to eight weeks for countries in the Caribbean Basin, depending on offshore location and transportation. The most serious drawback when investing in an 807 country, however, has to do with political risk. Many 807 countries rank extremely unfavorably in terms of potential political disruption and economic dislocation. There do exist stable countries with a reasonable risk profile, but the environment for risk in these countries has to be reevaluated periodically.

The major advantage of 807 sourcing is labor cost, since typical wage rates are generally 20 percent of U.S. wages. High labor content, therefore, is a critical criterion for 807 assembly. Although 807 operations currently are relatively small, they are expected to grow. By 1995, imports under the 807 provision may account for 10 percent of the nation's clothing sales, jumping from only 1.5 percent in 1984, according to Kurt Salmon Associates. Even apparel companies that make clothes primarily in the United States are considering 807 programs. They include Blue Bell's Wrangler Menswear division, based in Greensboro, North Carolina, which now imports only about 2 percent of its production. However, U.S. textile and apparel makers have generally been extremely reluctant to move production and employment offshore.

Other Government Programs

The U.S. government has other programs that are designed to improve the competitiveness of the domestic apparel and textile industries. In the late 1970s, the United States embarked upon a major long-term textile and apparel products export-expansion program. This formal program was inaugurated in early 1979 and was implemented by the Office of Textiles and Apparel in cooperation with the Commerce Department's Bureau of Export Development. However, because of the rapid increase in the value of the dollar, apparel is no longer competitive in many markets. The program is continuing, however, and is expected to show better results once the exchange rate of the dollar becomes better balanced with the currencies in Western Europe and in other countries where we made some significant gains in 1979 and 1980, before the dollar became so strong.

The Commerce Department also coordinated a major study of foreign sales potential for U.S. textiles and apparel in forty-seven countries around the world. This study has resulted in a number of proposed projects that could be undertaken to improve the industry's competitiveness and has led to a series of seminars for U.S. manufacturers which have been held in major cities in the United States.

In addition to these promotional campaigns, a number of other initiatives have been undertaken to improve the competitive environment for actual and potential exporters of textile products. The Commerce Department has examined the viability of developing U.S. export trading companies for textile and apparel products in order to encourage firms that believe themselves to be too small or unfamiliar with foreign trade to consider exporting. Export trading companies are now being formed and should expand their ability to export textiles and apparel as the dollar regains better equilibrium among world currencies.

The Corporate Response

New Sourcing Mixes

Companies, especially those in the apparel industry, have been actively investigating new sourcing mixes in an effort to improve competitiveness. Outside of the 807 program, options that have been pursued include domestic contracting; domestic production using foreign fabric; foreign contracting using either foreign or domestic fabric; and American-owned production overseas. These options have been used singly and in combination.

Domestic contracting is the oldest option available to apparel makers, and there are many advantages associated with it. By fulfilling all or part of the production requirements, domestic contracting reduces assets and staffing needs. It allows for the orderly buildup of domestic production while maintaining sales. It lowers overhead cost per unit because, when used as a way of handling peak production demand, it ensures that production facilities at normal levels of operation will function at maximum capacity for a maximum number of hours. Domestic contracting is also useful for handling styles or items that are not compatible with current production. Industry estimates that approximately 15 to 20 percent of all domestically produced goods are generated in contractor shops. Domestic contracting is a highly reliable source of quality work and provides excellent control of product flow. However, domestic-contractor sourcing generally adds to the garment cost.

Using foreign fabric in domestic production offers manufacturers generally about the same range of quality and reliability in delivery offered by U.S. textile makers. An advantage is that fabric can often be bought from overseas suppliers, who sometimes represent relatively small firms, in smaller lots; however, political instability or export restrictions may result in partially filled orders.

A domestic manufacturer can turn to a foreign contractor to perform a variety of tasks. In some cases, the contractor produces the fabric or yarn and produces the garments; in other cases, he or she buys the fabric and provides the package. Generally speaking, quality production is available from foreign sources, but the implementation of quality control is complex because of distance, language barriers, and the need to work through middlemen or agents. Furthermore, a number of factors outside the manufacturer's control, such as overloaded plants, shortage of operators, low productivity, and absenteeism, may interrupt shipments. Imported materials are also subject to quota restriction or embargoes; political upheaval; limits on shipping space; customs clearance holdups; utility breakdowns; and capricious acts of foreign governments. Consequently, lead times for foreign production are longer than for domestic production, which hinders flexibility. However, product costs are cut, and the investment required is less than that required for domestic production or in 807 operations.

The foreign production of garments in company-owned foreign plants includes joint-venture operations as well as manufacturer-owned plants. This alternative represents a small but growing portion of present sourcing arrangements. Quality control under this arrangement is more easily accomplished than when dealing with foreign contractors. The cost of building and equipping the plant raises considerably the investment required for company-owned foreign plants, but the product cost from owned plants should be less than comparable costs from a foreign contractor. There are other benefits associated with foreign ownership or joint venture. In many cases, such an arrangement will assure quota and favorable government treatment as well as tax advantages.

The reliance on various kinds of foreign sourcing has increased significantly in recent years. Kurt Salmon Associates estimates that apparel concerns currently import about 20 percent, or $11.5 billion of their brand name products, more than twice as much as five years ago. Much of these imports stem from nontraditional firms such as Calvin Klein, Ralph Lauren, and other brand names that source almost exclusively offshore. The share of their product mix accounted for by imports is expected to reach 35 percent by 1995.

Investment in Technology

While expansion of capacity in the U.S. textile and apparel industries has been limited in recent years, substantial outlays have been made for new plants and equipment designed to increase manufacturing efficiency and versatility. In addition to reducing production costs and improving the quality of fabrics, the newer technology also permits the manufacture of more complicated products with shorter start-up times. Most of the manufacturing breakthroughs in the textile complex have occurred because of technological improvements introduced by textile machinery firms, primarily those in West Germany, Switzerland, and Japan. Although this trend has made U.S. firms dependent on foreign textile-machinery manufacturers, industry leaders do not see this dependence as a disadvantage. As one said recently, "No other country, including the countries where they are produced, uses these machines as productively as the U.S."

In textiles, large investments have been made to automate chute feeders of fibers, to increase spinning speeds, and for the automatic doffer. Installation of open-end spinning equipment was expanded during the 1970s, since it offered reduced labor costs, improved yarn quality, and better uniformity. Open-end spinning boosts the rate of production four times over the older ring-spinning technique, reducing the number of steps involved in manufacturing some kinds of yarn from as many as fifteen to as few as three. The acceptance of the shuttleless loom also accelerated in recent years. Figures released by Adolf Sauer reveal that one-third of the weaving machines in operation in 1984 were shuttleless. These looms are faster and provide capabilities and a degree of flexibility not available in shuttle looms. They yield three times the speed of the latter, yet can produce seven to eight times the fabric because they weave wider widths. They are also safer and much quieter, better satisfying OSHA regulations, and they require less floor space than conventional looms. Most major weaving mills have also introduced computer-monitoring systems to increase their operating efficiency and loom productivity.

The cost of this new technology has increased sharply since the 1960s, limiting it to large and/or financially strong firms, a factor that has led to increased concentration in the textile industry. The combination of inflation and upgrading of machinery during the 1970s helped to boost spending for textile plant and equipment. Outlays rose from $800 million in 1970 to $1.18 billion by 1977 and reached a record $1.92 billion in 1984. Capital expenditures by the larger companies have far exceeded the annual provision for depreciation. The excess outlays must come from retained earnings or from borrowings. These innovations, however, have made U.S. firms more competitive. During the past decade, textile mills achieved an annual 3.5 percent increase in output per worker, versus a 2.3 percent increase for all U.S. manufacturing. Productivity in the apparel industry is now increasing by 4 percent annually, again owing to the introduction of automation.

It is estimated that the apparel industry was only 5 percent automated in the early 1960s. By the early 1970s the figure reached 15 percent. Aided by rapid development of electronics and miniaturization, automation reached some 25 percent during the 1970s and is now around 40 percent. Further progress is expected to be slow and costly. Furthermore, given the high cost of machinery, only a few large firms have been able to take advantage of these advances. Nonetheless, according to *Industry Week*, productivity in the apparel industry is now increasing by 4 percent annually.

Work-space management systems and technology such as laser cutting and computer-assisted pocket setting and stitching systems have been introduced. Computer-aided garment design is now a reality, and automated marker-making systems are used by most manufacturers. Major experiments in automation are being conducted by the Tailored Clothing Technology Corporation, a nonprofit research company sponsored by industry and labor groups.

Investment in technology has also produced dramatic results with the introduction of new distribution systems and methods. Computerized information systems are being used to run automated order processing, warehouse, and shipping activities. The benefits are lower costs and faster service. In one notable example, a major fiber company, a fabric company, and an apparel company linked their order entry, production scheduling, and distribution-management systems to a major retailer's computer. As a result of improved communications, these vendors were able to reduce the retailer's inventory levels by over 50 percent and reduce average response time on an order from over thirty days to about five days. As a result, the retailer was able to reduce dramatically the amount of product that had to be marked down or liquidated. Such investments in technology offer an opportunity for domestic suppliers to differentiate themselves from foreign vendors.

Specialization in the Textile and Apparel Industries

One of the primary goals of these modernization efforts has been to increase the competitiveness of the U.S. industry by increasing specialization in segments where it enjoys a leadership position and has strong market acceptance. Although attempts in the early 1980s to achieve specialization were hampered by the severe recessionary climate, as economic conditions improved, the textile and apparel industries were able to introduce new and improved products.

In recent years, leading apparel companies have been striving to increase their share of the market in fashion apparel. These efforts benefited from the strong demand sparked by the rebound in economic activity. In the women's area, the promising sectors include softer fashion sportswear, active wear, dresses, and lingerie. Suppliers to the men's market will be emphasizing woven dress shirts, tailored clothing, sportswear, and accessories. Best sellers in active-wear items have been warmup suits and heavier-weight jackets.

The U.S. textile industry has targeted the home furnishings market because of its belief that most product lines in this field offer long-term growth, are less volatile than most apparel markets, and are less subject to import competition. Shipments by furniture manufacturers increased by 22 percent in 1983, and orders for upholstery material and bedding increased accordingly. Shipments of carpets and rugs expanded as well in response to an upturn in housing and renovating. Slower growth in both these areas has been experienced in 1985, partly as a result of a slowing in housing starts. Automation, however, has been instrumental in helping American producers create vigorous niches in these areas. In large-scale carpet making for hotels and other public places, American producers, using computerized machinery, are capable of weaving with little setup time exact replacements for worn segments of carpet they had woven, and they are able to weave a series of such sections for different carpets in an almost unbroken sequence.

Another promising market being tapped by major textile mills is an area defined as industrial and other consumer products. This market grew from 23.0 percent of total fiber use in 1975 to 29.0 percent in 1983.

Important growth markets have been in medical, surgical, and sanitary applications, hose and belting, electrical and reinforced plastics, felts and filtration fabrics, bags and bagging, and coated and protective fabrics. Miscellaneous end uses that have shown a wide improvement include abrasives, book binding, luggage and handbags, shoes and slippers, tobacco cloth, wiping cloths and wall-covering fabrics, roofing materials, and wallboard and plaster applications. An important market for some mills is transportation fabrics, which include auto-seat upholstery, slipcovers, sidewall, headlining, and sheeting.

Many mills with a position in industrial fabrics have eliminated equipment that produces commodity-type goods and have upgraded their mix to include engineered fabrics for specific performance in various growing industrial areas. In 1985, J.P. Stevens put four of its five apparel-fabrics divisions up for sale. They comprise eighteen plants in four states, nearly seventy-five hundred employees, and 1984 sales of $559.4 million. In the meantime, Stevens has proceeded with its plans to start a new auto-carpet plant in Port Huron, Michigan, capable of producing, packaging, and shipping auto carpet to arrive two to six hours before it is due to be installed in General Motors automobiles. Stevens's new factory illustrates a trend that will become increasingly important in the textile and apparel industries and that has important implications for the manufacturing sector as a whole: the establishment of close coordination between suppliers and customers from different industries. The arrangement between Stevens and General Motors cuts response time and eliminates the need for costly warehousing, thus resulting in considerable savings for both parties.

Recent Strategies Pursued by Retailers

American retailers have turned to overseas suppliers in an effort to offer low-priced merchandise in an increasingly congested domestic market. In some instances, retailers even maintain permanent facilities and permanent staffs abroad to assure a supply of low-cost goods. Market conditions have also led retailers, in an effort to create a market "niche," to become increasingly involved in the manufacture of apparel that they import. Until recently, retailers imported apparel that essentially copied the styles and fashions generated by the domestic-apparel industry. Some retailers now are doing their own styling and designing, in addition to developing garment specifications, hiring contractors, and arranging for the packaging and shipping of merchandise to their stores. In effect, the retailing industry has assumed some of the traditional functions of its manufacturing vendors. Critics of this move maintain that the primary reason for this shift is that retailers can mark up cheaper imported goods more than they can domestic goods and still remain competitive. The retailers, however, cite a recent study compiled by the Nathan Katz Company which revealed that gross margins for imports were not appreciably higher than on domestically produced goods and that this slight advantage was offset by operating, logistics and merchandising costs. Spokesmen for the retail industry maintain that they would prefer to do business with American firms but find it difficult to locate manufacturers who are willing to assume the shorter runs associated with their specialty lines.

The Consequences of Governmental and Corporate Policy

The U.S. textile and apparel industries have made extensive efforts to adjust to the increasing competition from abroad, and during the 1970s, this adjustment process, at least in the textile industry, proceeded relatively smoothly. Agreements with foreign governments made under the guidelines established by the MFA by no means stopped the growth of imports but kept it within levels that encouraged the industry to adjust. The apparel industry, though it fared less well, was subject to pressure from imports that increased at moderate levels. Both industries performed relatively well in comparison to their OECD counterparts. However, in the 1980s, the nature of the worldwide marketplace changed dramatically. The stability of the domestic textile and apparel industries, as well as the stability of the domestic market for textiles and apparels, was undermined by a flood of imports.

One immediate reason for the rise in imports, as we have noted, is the rise of the dollar to unprecedented levels, which caused rising import from both NICs and other OECD nations at the same time that it tended to divert additional NIC products from the OECD to the U.S. market. But more fundamental has been the change in the character of the international market, which has been marked by the arrival of the NIC as important and permanent participants. Much of the sense of crisis that pervades the textile and apparel industries as well as the retailing industry has to do with the problem of adjusting government and corporate policy to reflect conditions that are unprecedented. The strategies that have been adopted in the past have generally worked in the past, but the time has come to adopt strategies that reflect present conditions. If this is not done, then we stand to lose large segments of these industries, which once lost will not easily be regenerated. The implications of such decisions, however, extend far beyond the textile and apparel industries to other sectors whose performance has been hampered by competition from imports. In essence, the debate that currently centers on strategies for the textile and apparel industries is crucial to the fate of our manufacturing sector as a whole. The central issue revolves around the speed and nature of the adjustment process.

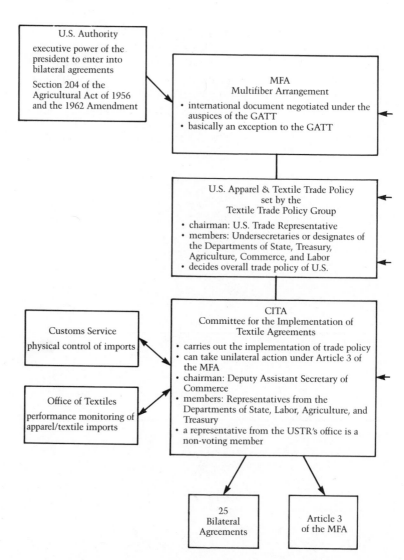

Figure 4–1. Administration of Trade Policy

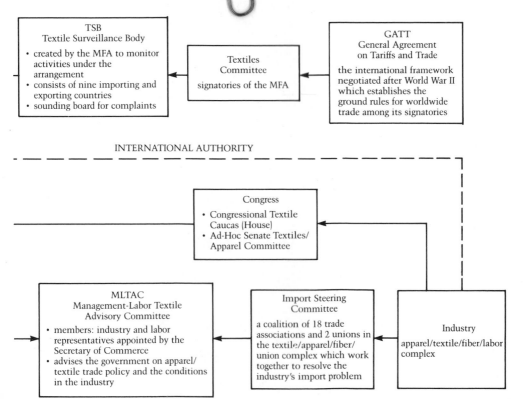

TSB
Textile Surveillance Body

- created by the MFA to monitor activities under the arrangement
- consists of nine importing and exporting countries
- sounding board for complaints

Textiles Committee

signatories of the MFA

GATT
General Agreement on Tariffs and Trade

the international framework negotiated after World War II which establishes the ground rules for worldwide trade among its signatories

INTERNATIONAL AUTHORITY

Congress

- Congressional Textile Caucas (House)
- Ad-Hoc Senate Textiles/ Apparel Committee

MLTAC
Management-Labor Textile Advisory Committee

- members: industry and labor representatives appointed by the Secretary of Commerce
- advises the government on apparel/ textile trade policy and the conditions in the industry

Import Steering Committee

a coalition of 18 trade associations and 2 unions in the textile/apparel/fiber/ union complex which work together to resolve the industry's import problem

Industry

apparel/textile/fiber/labor complex

Item	Stat. Suffix	Articles	Units of Quantity	Rates of Duty	
				1	2
807.00	00	Articles assembled abroad in whole or in part of fabricated components, the product of the United States, which (a) were exported in condition ready for assembly without further fabrication, (b) have not lost their physical identity in such articles by change in form, shape, or otherwise, and (c) have not been advanced in value or improved in condition abroad except by being assembled and except by operations incidental to the assembly process such as cleaning, lubricating, and painting	1/ 2/	A duty upon the full value of the imported article, less the cost or value of such products of the United States (see headnote 3 of this subpart)	A duty upon the full value of the imported article, less the cost or value of such products of the United States (see headnote 3 of this subpart)

Source: *Tariff Schedules of the United States Annotated (1984).* Schedule 8: Special Classification Provisions. Part 1: Articles Exported and Returned.

Figure 4–2. Item 807 of the Tariff Schedules of the United States

5
Proposals for Restoring U.S. Competitiveness

A number of trends will affect the competitiveness of U.S. industry on world markets. The market for manufactured goods is growing in real terms, especially among the developing nations. The emergence of the NICs, as we have seen, has challenged the preeminence of the developed countries on the world markets, but the NICs are consumers as well as producers, and their markets can be expected to become more receptive to foreign goods as their domestic industries grow in strength. There is also a second tier of nations, both in Asia and in South America, which can be expected to become important markets for manufactured products. Growth in most developing-nation markets is, however, predicated on the resolution of the substantial debt and foreign exchange problems that face them.

Markets in the developed world will continue to grow, but not at the rate that will characterize the rest of the world. A more significant factor in the development of these markets, and one that has already distinguished them, is the "aging" of their populations. This shift can create important opportunities for producers. For instance, although the population of the United States itself will increase by 12 percent (or by 28 million people) between 1982 and 1995, the overall change is not as important as the changes within each age-group market. The most significant shift that is expected in the population is the substantial growth in households headed by members of the thirty-five-to-fifty-four age bracket and the decline in the young adult population by about 22 percent. The real issue is, Who will benefit from these trends—domestic or foreign producers?

The effects that these changes will have on the textile and apparel industries are clear. Worldwide consumption of textiles and textile products is projected to grow by 50 percent over the next fifteen years, with most of that expansion occurring outside the United States, in the developing nations. The demand for manmade fibers will continue to increase faster than the demand for natural fibers.

The expected rise in the standard of living in such advanced developing countries as Brazil will be a major force behind the increased demand for textiles and textile products. While its basic apparel needs may be satisfied by domestic production, Brazil may well become a major importer of more sophisticated apparel. Other Latin American nations, such as Mexico, Argentina, Chile, Venezuela, and Colombia, if they can manage their debt burdens, are expected to increase their standard of living over the next five to ten years as well. In the Far East, Korea and Taiwan may also become a market for specialized U.S. goods as trade barriers are removed.

In the United States, the maturing of the baby boomers will continue to have a considerable impact on consumer demand for textiles and apparel. Between 1982 and 1995, the growth in the children's market—ages three to seven—will be about 20 percent in total. The young adult population will actually decline, but by 1995, the number of people between thirty-five and forty-four will increase by 49 percent and the age group between forty-five and fifty-four will grow by 40 percent. These two age groups will affect apparel and textile demand more than any other portion of the population. Together, the thirty-five-to-fifty-four-year age group will increase from 50.6 to 73.4 million and will represent 28 percent of the total population in 1995. They have different apparel needs than they did as young adults fifteen years ago, and they can be expected to spend more on these goods.

Another significant trend that will affect the textile and apparel industries is the increase in persons over age sixty-five. Between 1982 and 1995, the senior-citizen bracket will grow dramatically. Although members of this group will still represent only 12 to 13 percent of the total population, their numbers will grow by 7 million, to 33.9 million. Although many members of this group live on relatively low, fixed incomes, this group as a whole has the largest percent of savings. Although they do not represent the market for apparel that other age groups do, the growth in their population will coincide with a growth in demand for textile-based health-care products and materials. Other demographic changes in the United States will also affect the textile and apparel industries and create new opportunities for producers. Most notable among these are the shift in population to the Sunbelt—from Virginia south and southwest to California—and a projected increase in household formation. The implications of these changes is that within a slowly growing market, new market niches will continue to be created.

Improving U.S. Competitiveness

It would be both costly and damaging for the United States to try to recover the type of competitive position it enjoyed in the world economy in the 1950s and 1960s; indeed, such efforts would almost certainly result in failure. What is required, therefore, is a new definition of competitiveness, one founded on the ability to respond quickly to market conditions rather than on the power to dictate them. And here it is possible for the U.S. manufacturing sector to emerge as a strong force on world markets and to recover segments of the domestic market that it has lost to imports. Although the manufacturing sector has suffered declining competitiveness, not all indicators are gloomy. The United States is far from becoming a service economy. In 1983, for instance, employment in the manufacturing sector rose by 6 percent, more than the rate of increase of 2.4 percent in the service industries. And International Monetary Fund (IMF) statistics indicate that industrial production in April 1985 had increased by 13 percent over levels in 1980, a greater increase than those of any of our major competitors with the exception of Japan. These and other indicators suggest clearly that the U.S. industrial sector has not lost the capacity to recoup its competitiveness. In the following sections, we shall examine the steps that the textile and apparel industries propose to take to restore their competitiveness, along with changes in government policy that have been offered to further their efforts. In our conclusion, we shall discuss the implications that these proposals have for the manufacturing sector as a whole.

Corporate Options for Improving Competitiveness of the Textile and Apparel Industries

Any action on the part of U.S. textile and apparel manufacturers to increase the competitiveness of their products on the international markets needs to take into account the following factors:

1. the continued growth of the textile and apparel industry in the developing world
2. the rapid diffusion of technology to developing countries

3. projected demographic changes in the domestic and international markets

4. the costs and benefits of specialization and modernization

Although the issues are complex, there are several courses of action that would improve the position of the textile and apparel industries. The first is increased coordination between textile and apparel manufacturers and their suppliers and consumers. This involves an essential change in philosophy, which has already begun to occur in these industries. J.P. Stevens's effort to match automobile-carpet production to the demands of the General Motors assembly line entails close cooperation between both groups. Agreements such as this one result in substantial savings for both parties because they often involve shared responsibility for inventory and transportation and reduce warehouse requirements. Increased cooperation within the industry and between textile and apparel producers and the retailing industry could result in a decline in the import of apparel by retailers.

This type of cooperation is predicated upon improvements in the production process. The pace of modernization, especially in the textile industry, has been rapid. By the end of the decade, according to the Institute of Textile Technology, plants may require one-third fewer workers than in the 1970s. By 1990, an industrial fabric plant with a hundred sewing machines, five hundred employees, and five hundred industrial robots working multiple shifts could maintain the same level of production as a 1980 plant with two thousand sewing machines and twenty-five hundred employees working a single shift. But faster production in textiles or apparel is not an end in itself. Two other goals must be accomplished for the automation to be effective. It must allow the production of the kind of short runs required by retailers who need limited stocks of brand name merchandise, and it must allow for short setup time. These qualities have become of paramount importance, especially in the apparel industry, where changes in fashion have become more exacting and have been occurring at a rapidly increasing pace. There is considerable room for improvement in this area. Norman Hinerfeld of the Wingspread Corporation has pointed out that in the six-month product cycle necessary to design, produce, and deliver a shirt, only fifteen minutes is required for the actual production of that garment. Faster through-put time is not, however, a factor simply of increased automation. It requires new institutional relationships within organizations and between them.

The shorter response times and greater flexibility that changes in management philosophy and the implementation of new equipment can achieve, coupled with the reputation of American firms for producing high-quality merchandise, can go far, if conditions allow, in helping the textile and apparel industries stem the tide of imports and increase exports. Many of these changes have already begun to be implemented—J.P. Stevens reports that it has captured contracts to produce sheets that had formerly been produced abroad—and we can expect to see, in coming years, textile and apparel industries that have redefined their relationship to their suppliers and customers, that have placed greater emphasis on marketing, and that have identified and cultivated high-value-added niches.

Governmental Options for Improving the Competitiveness of the Textile and Apparel Industries

Given the present circumstances, some government action to allow the textile and apparel industries to achieve these changes, which, as we have seen, benefit other manufacturing sectors as well, is warranted. These actions must reflect short-term factors, such as the rise in the dollar, as well as the long-term change in the nature of the international marketplace. During the 1970s, the MFA and bilateral agreements negotiated under its guidelines provided an adequate means of permitting U.S. industry to adjust to changes in the international market. This, of course, all changed with the rise of the dollar, which was damaging of itself in terms of the balance of trade and because it stimulated exporting nations to circumvent U.S. textile and apparel import restrictions. The rise in the value of the dollar, however, only accelerated changes which had been occurring gradually throughout the period. Rolling the dollar back, while it will certainly provide a much-welcome boost to U.S. producers, will not undo the fundamental changes in the market which its rise has stimulated. Furthermore, such measures will be effective only if they include adjustment in relation to NIC currencies as well as to the currencies of other OECD nations.

Simple protectionism is not the answer. In the short run, protectionism drives up prices and dampens demand. In the long run, it tends dangerously to postpone the restructuring necessary to restore an industry's competitiveness. What is needed in the textile and apparel industries, therefore, is a mechanism that will encourage firms to adjust to the realities of the market while mitigating the distracting and often damaging effects of rapid and significant fluctuations in market conditions. The goal of such a governmental policy is to provide an environment in which textile and apparel firms, whose profit margins are relatively low, can pursue a policy of adjustment.

A major measure before Congress in 1985, H.R. 1562 and S. 680, respresented one approach to the problem. These bills, sponsored by Rep. Ed Jenkins of Georgia and 290 other congressmen and Sen. Strom Thurmond and 54 other senators, would have replaced the current system of bilateral agreements negotiated under the MFA with a statutory scheme of quotas imposed on all supplier countries (except Canada and the EEC) that would be much broader in product coverage (covering, for example, fibers such as silk, ramie, and linen, which are not now subject to restraint). Such a change to comprehensive, statutory formula would have eliminated the role of CITA in making market-disruption findings and calls for consultation.

The bill, as originally formulated, would have established a scheme of individual quotas for each product from each supplier country. The countries affected were divided into two categories: major exporting countries (those which supplied 1.25 percent or more of U.S. textile product imports during 1984) and smaller exporting countries. Export levels for the major exporting countries would have been cut back sharply and limited to 1 percent growth per year, while those of smaller exporting countries would have been set at higher levels and limited to 6 percent. Preliminary estimates indicated that the overall imports from the twelve major exporting countries would have been cut back by approximately 35 to 40 percent. Sensitive to charges that the measure was protectionistic, the textile industry asked that the number of major exporters be limited to the top three—Hong Kong, South Korea, and Taiwan. These three accounted for 35 percent of U.S. imports in 1984.

An important question that surrounds measures of this type is the extent to which they are consistent with our international obligations under the MFA. Defenders of the bill maintained that the bill did not represent a departure from this arrangement, which allows, under Article 3, an importing country to take unilateral action against imports under certain conditions. However, the unilateral quotas proposed in Congress, unlike those specified in the MFA, would have gone into effect without any prior consultation with supplier countries and would have been permanent in duration. Those who opposed the bill also found the costs to the American consumer to be prohibitive and the consequences for the retailing industry to be damaging. Other opponents feared retaliation against sectors like agriculture, aerospace, electronics, chemicals, and pharmaceuticals if the bill were to have been passed.

Congress passed this bill, only to see it vetoed by President Reagan. The issue is, however, far from dead. Attempts to override this veto in 1986 will depend on the outcome of the negotiations to renew the MFA.

Another proposal is for a movement away from the MFA system to a system of global quotas. Proponents of this view believe the present system has severe flaws. They cite the confrontational aspects of bilateral negotiations and describe the mechanisms used to address unfair trade practices as being detrimental to foreign relations. They also maintain that in countries in which the desire to export is greater than quota availability, the market price for export licenses drives up the price of merchandise. Furthermore, they believe that the present system creates divisiveness and controversy between importers and retailers and domestic producers, between Congress and the administration, and among various government agencies.

The solution they offer is the establishment of a limited global quota program for low-wage supplying countries. A major advantage of this system is that it would close off the loopholes that allow exporters to evade quota restrictions by shipping goods from countries that have not met their quota or that have no quota. Under this program, the government periodically would determine import levels for sensitive textile and apparel categories with an overall fixed growth rate determined periodically. As in the current system, growth rates in various categories of products could differ, based on the sensitivity of the domestic market and the degree of import penetration. Nonsensitive categories would be excluded from the program. In order to guard against a country adopting predatory pricing practices in an attempt to dominate the market, no single supplying country would be allowed to supply more than a fixed percent of the market. In fact, one of the advantages of such a program, the proponents of this plan maintain, is that it could be used to promote production in the needier suppliers. They offer several ways of administering the program. Import licenses could be issued on a first-come, first-served basis, or the quota could be auctioned off periodically.

A consistent objection raised to such a quota system and other plans like it is that quotas increase the burden on the American consumer. Other critics argue that this plan does not really address the problems it is designed to solve. It depends on negotiations between government agencies and between producers and importers and retailers to determine the growth rates of sensitive categories. There is little likelihood that the discord created by this process will differ markedly from that which presently accompanies the administration of the MFA.

Another view is that the MFA provides an adequate mechanism for promoting adjustments to the changing international market and should not be abandoned. Many of the supporters of this view, among them Stanley Nehmer and Mark W. Love of Economic Consulting Services, advocate supplementing the bilateral agreements with global import ceilings, at least for the most sensitive products, to reduce surges. Levels under the bilateral agreements could be subsumed under the global ceilings. Supporters also argue for the restoration of overall and group ceilings in bilateral agreements with individual countries and the institution of import licensing to replace the current reliance on foreign-government export controls. The ability to control unexpected, sharp surges in imports, assuming adequate domestic capacity, should be part of any trade policy solution in this and other industries.

Related Measures Necessary for the Success of Corporate and Governmental Options for the Textile and Apparel Industries

To be successful, the corporate options pursued to restructure these industries and the government options taken to control the influx of imports must be integrated with a series of measures taken in a number of related areas. We will mention only the most salient of these. Of paramount importance is that steps be taken to control or neutralize the trade effects of any rise in the value of the dollar, a condition that has exacerbated the difference between U.S. wage scales and those in developing countries. The 80 percent rise in the value of the dollar during the decade has accelerated changes in the market and has created changes in the manufacturing sectors of other industrialized countries as well as in the developing nations, changes that in the long term could prove to be a liability. In the textile and apparel industries, the rise in the dollar can be directly linked to the immediate drop in U.S. exports that were priced out of foreign markets and the unprecedented surge in imports which developed in the eighteen-to-twenty-four-month period that followed. The present level of the dollar and the uncertainty of current economic trends make it very difficult for the industries to continue to carry out their plans for adjustment and modernization. While the dollar has declined relative to other developed nations, it remains at historic highs in relation to the currency of major NIC textile importers.

The factors contributing to the strong dollar are numerous, complex, and intertwined. Stated briefly, the United States is currently considered to be a safe haven for investment because of its large and growing economy, its political stability, and its recognized position as a world leader. Second, the U.S. economy has recovered from the last recession sooner and at a faster rate than the other economies of the world. The resultant expectation of greater growth in the United States attracts foreign interests. Third, during the past few years there has been a large net capital inflow into the United States, which has added to the strength of the dollar. This is primarily attributed to cutbacks by domestic banks on loans to developing countries. Finally, real interest rates are high compared with interest rates of other countries.

Reducing the interest rates has been one focus of recent efforts to control the trade deficits, and controlling the federal deficit, the primary reason that interest rates are so high, is the obvious solution. In 1984, outstanding federal borrowing was nearly 48 percent of the total net demand for credit. Resolving the budget crisis will be a long and difficult process. Recently, however, there has been greater capital outflow from the United States, thus causing a small but noticeable drop in the dollar against foreign currencies.

Another approach is the one recently taken by the Reagan administration. The finance ministers from the five largest industrial democracies agreed in September 1985 to intervene in foreign-exchange markets to bring down the price of the dollar. Commentators believe that regular intervention could reduce the volatile swings in the price of the dollar which have plagued international finance and trade since 1973, when the United States and its major trading partners abandoned fixed exchange rates and allowed money prices to float. But since these efforts have so far resulted only in a modest decrease in the price of the dollar against our OECD trading partners and not against the NICs, they have had little impact on the textile and apparel industries.

The textile and apparel industries would also be aided by efforts to promote U.S. exports. One suggestion is that the United States implement agreements with selected foreign governments to provide reciprocal access of markets. Agreements of this sort would be particularly appropriate with major exporters such as South Korea, Hong Kong, Taiwan, and China. Such agreements, to be successful, would need to be accompanied by federal programs to encourage American textile and apparel producers to enter the export trade. Another appropriate topic that falls under the heading of tax reform and trade policy reform is the role of automation incentives in supporting industries in the international market. Such incentives could hasten adjustment and improve competitiveness and performance.

A final area in which reforms need to be made if there is to be increased cooperation between the textile and apparel industries and their suppliers and consumers is the field of antitrust. George C. Lodge and William C. Crum have written that "past anti-trust standards have apparently deterred export activities, discouraged industry cooperation, and failed to adequately reflect the effects of foreign competition when evaluating combinations of domestic firms seeking economies of scale." This situation needs to be remedied. Recently, the Reagan administration has allowed textile and apparel companies to specialize in specific product lines in order to gain major market shares without antitrust suits.

6

U.S. Industry in International Competition: Lessons from the Textile and Apparel Industries

The textile and apparel industries provide an important source of insight into the problems that threaten the U.S. industrial sector. Other sectors have begun to experience the severe international competition that this industry has faced for decades. In some respects, the industry has performed admirably, yet its future remains uncertain. The impact of international competition in textiles and apparel and its effect on workers, managers, suppliers, investors, and customers hold important lessons for virtually all other American manufacturing industries.

There are several factors unique to these two industries which have made the past five years particularly difficult. Textiles and apparel are relatively price-sensitive, and manufacturers realize limited operating margins. Currency movements, consequently, have a relatively large impact on performance. Currency shifts of even 5 to 10 percent can restrict a vendor's pricing flexibility and can eliminate profits. The strong U.S. dollar in the first half of the 1980s hit the textile and apparel industries especially hard.

The textile industry also faced particularly intense pressure because of its status in the economic development programs of the NICs. Apparel, in particular, often plays a leading role in the early stages of industrialization. During this stage of national economic development, the industry frequently represents the primary source of foreign exchange. Countries such as Hong Kong, Taiwan, and Korea have committed substantial resources and support to their domestic textile industries, and they vigorously pursue a policy of exporting much of their output. The recent rapid expansion of export-oriented textile production capacity in these and other NICs has contributed greatly to the U.S. industries' problems.

But although the textile and apparel industries have been hard hit by competition from the NICs, many industries across the manufacturing sector have felt pressure from the NICs. This is because the NICs have continued to upgrade their manufacturing activities to include higher-value-added industries. Ten years ago, Korea was exporting shirts; now it is exporting Hyundais. If there is one area in which the textile industry does stand alone, it is in facing competition from China. Yet, inevitably, China will eventually become a player in other industrial sectors.

Because the textile and apparel industries have been the first to bear the brunt of international competition, they were also the first to benefit from U.S. trade policy. The Multifiber Arrangement has provided a partial buffer against foreign competition, and interest in this type of trade regulation as a prototype for other industries has grown. The MFA seemed to work well in the 1970s, permitting controlled import growth, continued consumer benefits, and orderly restructuring and improvements in industrial efficiency. In the past five years, however, textile imports have surged, rising above the levels indicated in the MFA guidelines.

Industrial Responses

The typical U.S. textile company in 1987 finds itself in far worse financial condition than at any time in recent history. Rates of bankruptcy in the industry have reached unprecedented levels. The industry faces ongoing pressure to reduce costs, improve quality, increase service, develop new markets, diversify, and otherwise differentiate itself from its foreign competitors. These efforts have been going on for some time and will be continued. Given the industry's size and scope, it has produced a wide array of responses and initiatives, many of which have added a spot of light to an otherwise gloomy outlook.

The general thrust of these initiatives may provide possible vehicles for improving competitiveness in other industries. The textile and apparel industries have taken steps to increase labor productivity through automation and have lowered indirect overhead costs. This strategy, which most straightforwardly addressed the problem, has been successful in many instances. In addition, several other new response patterns have emerged which promise to have a significant impact on the industry and which could be adopted by other sectors as well. It is worthwhile to highlight once again both the traditional and innovative strategies that have been used, because these represent the steps that large segments of the U.S. manufacturing sector can contemplate in the next few years.

Privatization

The textile and apparel industries have always had a tradition of private ownership. Many large firms, such as Milliken, have been in private hands since they were founded. A recent trend has been the return of publicly owned companies to private ownership. In recent years, such prominent firms such as Levi Strauss, Cannon Mill, and Riegle Textiles were taken private in management buyouts. The growing prevalence of private ownership may provide greater flexibility and competitiveness to these firms. The increase in fixed-debt payments for highly leveraged concerns can work to reduce flexibility, of course, but as principal is repaid, these firms will increase their flexibility and capital investment. Privatization can eliminate dividend payout, reduce reporting requirements, speed management decision making, and increase responsiveness. In many instances, leveraged buyouts may include employee-ownership participation. Employee Share Ownership Plans (ESOPs) have been used to finance buyouts in a number of instances. Most notably, ESOP funds provided the primary capital source for the takeover of Dan River Mills. The use of ESOPs reduces the financial pressures on management which usually follow privatization, and employee ownership is especially beneficial when combined with the new industrial-relations programs. Industrial-relations programs, including Scanlon plans, quality circle systems, and other employee-participation and incentive programs have been widely adopted throughout the industry. These programs have contributed to notable improvements in quality and productivity and have led to reductions in inventory, response time, and overhead.

Divestment and Diversification

As we have noted, the hardest-hit segment of the textile industry has been apparel. Bankruptcy rates have been high, and many firms have disposed of their apparel operations. One such company was J.P. Stevens, which sold its apparel division in 1985. Such sales reflect a shift by fabric makers away from the apparel market. Because domestic-apparel production has shrunk, fabric makers have begun to emphasize other downstream markets, like carpeting and industrial products. Other firms in the textile industry have diversified. DuPont, the primary supplier of synthetic fibers, has stepped up its production of specialty chemicals and electronics. At the same time, Milliken has moved into agricultural chemicals and detergents. The apparel makers have also increased specialization. They have pursued niches in high-fashion goods and in areas that are relatively sheltered from the thrust of import penetration. Such a niche strategy allows a company to hold a large percentage of market share and develop a high degree of brand identification.

New Products and New Methods

Relentless international pressure on existing products has stimulated firms to create and introduce new products. Several recent successes can be cited, although they did not all originate in the mainstream textile industry. Goretex, a fabric used in sporting goods and specialty applications, including surgery, is the basis for a new line of premium-priced outdoor apparel. Lycra, recently introduced by Milliken, is another fabric that has caught on with the sports-minded consumer because of its excellent wash-and-wear qualities. There have also been advances in stain-resistant fabrics as well as nonwicking and wicking apparel for specialty uses. An important development in the industrial area is synthetic asbestos, recently introduced by a New York company, which poses none of the health hazards of natural asbestos.

In addition to the introduction of new products, the textile industry has concentrated on achieving significant improvement in production processes. Great efforts have been made to improve defect rates in the fabric industry. Reduction in the number of defects per square yard of fabric permit apparel makers to work with larger pieces of fabric, thereby easing assembly and reducing the amount of apparel that is subject to markdowns. The financial condition of the apparel industry has not permitted the same level of investment found in the fiber and fabric sectors, but process innovations have occurred in this segment as well. Apparel makers have installed new equipment, which has contributed to cost and quality improvements. One particularly interesting example is Kayser-Roth's use of new knitting technology to produce high-fashion sweaters on short notice.

Outsourcing

The growing use of independent foreign suppliers to displace domestic production sources is occurring throughout U.S. industry. Concern about the viability of "hollow corporations" has been expressed in many forums. But, as we have seen, the U.S. textile industry, as it has been traditionally conceived, has not relied heavily on outsourcing. A number of the new entrants in the industry, on the other hand, have been extremely active in this area. This phenomenon has been particularly significant in brand name or licensed apparel. Such lines as Calvin Klein, Ralph Lauren, Liz Claiborne, Lacoste, and Yves St. Laurent typically focus on design, marketing, and promotion, leaving the manufacturing to independent contractors. In some cases, retailers also develop close ties with foreign manufacturers, who then produce apparel to the retailers' specifications. The products are then sold under a captive brand controlled by the retailer.

Outsourcing is significant because a large percentage of recent apparel-import growth has occurred in these two areas. Furthermore, outsourcing is expected to become more prevalent in coming years. The recent devaluation of the Mexican peso has greatly reduced the cost of assembly facilities in Mexico. The Mexican border zone, an area that permits manufacturers to import components from the United States and reexport assembled goods back into the country without duties or tariffs, offers a low-cost, geographically convenient base for outsourcing activities. It is likely that the Caribbean will be used increasingly as well.

However, domestic production in many areas remains strong, and not all best-selling brands are made overseas. In the towel market, Cannon, Fieldcrest, and Royal brands dominate, while Jockey, BVD, Hanes, and Fruit of the Loom account for most of the men's underwear market. Levis, Wrangler, and Blue Bell denim products dominate another apparel segment. In each of these cases, the brand name is backed up by domestic production.

Advertising and Promotion

Several industry-wide promotion campaigns have attempted to establish a greater public awareness of international competition and to develop a preference for apparel produced in the United States. The International Ladies Garment Workers Union sponsored a series of advertisements around the "Look for the union label" slogan. More recently, the textile industry sponsored a $100 million labeling drive featuring the phrase "Crafted with pride in the U.S.A." Although the success of such "made in America" programs has been limited in the past, several indicators suggest that consumer responsiveness to such themes may be rising. A 1986 *Money* magazine survey revealed that 80 percent of U.S. consumers preferred a domestic product, everything else being equal. More importantly, over half of those consumers with an annual income of less than $15,000 and a third of consumers with incomes over this amount reported that they were actually shifting their spending from imported items to domestic products.

New Responses

The textile industry has tried all the traditional responses to foreign competition, and although they have produced some significant successes, these methods alone are not adequate to a crisis of the magnitude that faces the textile and apparel industries. The industries have been driven to explore new approaches, some of which hold high promise of relief.

The textile and apparel industries are somewhat unique in the development of captive retail chains. Levi Strauss has been most active in expanding its direct retail presence, although other textile firms also control captive retail outlets. Perhaps more important than direct retail operation, however, is the development of the new relationship between textile vendors and independent retailers. The use of new computer and communications technologies to manage these relationships represents a crucial breakthrough.

As we have shown, these computerized communications links permit real-time communication between vendors and customers, thus shortening delivery cycles and improving customer service and satisfaction. Such a system was installed in 1985 to link DuPont's fiber division, J.P. Stevens's fabric unit, several apparel makers, and J.C. Penney's retail operations. An electronic order from the retailer immediately triggered deliveries by suppliers at all three levels of the production chain. By instituting real-time delivery systems, these firms found that they were able to reduce the inventory in the chain by about two-thirds, with most of the benefit going to the retailer. In addition, the labor and overhead costs associated with order processing, inventory management, and logistics were reduced by more than half throughout the chain. The average response time for delivery of ordered goods went from over thirty days to under five.

An integrated production chain linked by computers is a particularly effective way of meeting the challenge of foreign competition. It links supplier-consumer relationships in such a way as to virtually exclude other partners. And since foreign vendors typically have the longest lead time and the least-liberal return policies, they are rarely chosen for inclusion in such a system.

A second initiative that depends on technology also favors domestic producers. Flexible manufacturing systems, especially when combined with the networks described above, are an important source of competitive advantage. The underlying goal of these systems is to allow rapid, low-cost setup for a variety of different products. Furthermore, these systems offer design capabilities as well. Customers can specify design features, which are then stored electronically for future retrieval. For instance, Milliken's institutional carpet line offers essentially unlimited design options and allows for replacement of any section of the carpet after it becomes worn. Foreign producers rarely have the capital to pursue such innovations.

Flexible manufacturing systems are being studied and adopted by the U.S. textile and apparel industries. The rapid response and delivery systems that American producers can put into place are viewed as an important weapon against foreign competition. These methods can also be adapted by other industries as well.

Nonmanagement Factors

The textile industry's efforts to respond to foreign competition trace a pattern that is appearing with increasing frequency in other industries. Management reduced costs by cutting employment and limiting wage and salary increases, and it automated some plants and closed others. Marginal product lines were dropped or sold. Many firms turned to outsourcing, relying on low-cost foreign components or finished goods.

Increased emphasis on marketing and distribution activity is a strategy the textile industry has also pursued. Branding and advertising activity have been used as a means of differentiating product offering, while U.S. vendors have stressed service to retail customers, rapid response time, full-line product offering, customized design, favorable credit terms, and quick delivery. Domestic distributors of foreign products cannot readily provide comparable services.

Although management in the textile industry has made significant steps toward reducing costs, improving quality, and enhancing service, these initiatives have not stemmed the growth of textile imports. The lesson to be learned from this situation is clear. Management response of itself cannot enable the U.S. textile industry to retain a competitive position because many of the conditions that have determined recent market developments are beyond management control.

It has become painfully obvious in recent years that the presumed relationship between foreign exchange rates and trade activity has been at least temporarily suspended. Although the United States ran huge trade deficits in the first half of the 1980s, its currency appreciated against those of its major trading partners. The capital flows that now dominate foreign exchange markets have led to substantial imbalances in trade activity which have greatly injured U.S. industry. Even a 30 to 40 percent shift in exchange rates can undo the most innovative management effort to improve competitiveness.

The 1986 decline in the value of the dollar will eventually reverse trade patterns with respect to Europe. However, Europe accounts for only a small fraction of U.S. textile trade deficit. The primary textile exporters—Korea, Taiwan, India, China, and other NICs—have not experienced exchange-rate shifts.

Other factors that cannot be combated by more efficient or resourceful domestic management and that improve the competitive position of these countries include export tax rebates, subsidies, preferential financing, and protected home markets. These structural supports increase the role of nonmanagerial variables in industrial competition. Any comprehensive attempt to improve the competitiveness of the U.S. textile industry or the entire manufacturing sector must take these factors into account.

Implications for Public Policy

The textile industry's recent experience underscores several key issues that will affect the U.S. economy. First, there is a very high degree of interdependence within the U.S. industrial sector. As we have seen in the textile industry, problems in the apparel segment rapidly produced problems for fiber and fabric producers. This is true for the entire industrial sector as well. Econometric models and input-output matrices show the precise interrelationships between different industrial segments. A reduction of output in any U.S. industry results in a specific reduction in the shipments of other industries. Reductions in automobile production, for instance, result in lower shipments in glass, steel, plastic, and rubber. Displacement due to foreign competition is felt throughout the economy.

Second, sustained misalignment of currency values has permanent effects. Prolonged exposure to overvalued exchange rates can irreversibly damage industry infrastructure. The damage is not automatically repaired when the exchange rates become more properly aligned. Such capacity cannot be reestablished—if it is to be reestablished at all—without significant cost and investment.

Third, combating international industrial competition is not the sole responsibility of the private sector. Public promotion and protection must play a vital role. In the United States and other industrial countries, the textile industry does not exhibit levels of public intervention as pronounced as in industries such as aerospace, agriculture, shipbuilding, and telecommunications. It is, however, the object of significant public activity in the developing economies.

The Industrial Outlook

If shipments grow for a specific industry, the result is increased orders for suppliers to that industry, who in turn increase their purchases of components and capital equipment. As more and more purchases of consumer goods shift overseas, this multiplier effect is lost. A fraction of the multiplier effect can be regained if foreign producers purchase part of their requirements from U.S. vendors, but that fraction will generally be very small. To the extent that foreign producers are served in their home markets by local affiliates of U.S. companies, the multiplier effect is further reduced.

From a macroeconomic perspective, the U.S. economy has been losing, or exporting, its multiplier effect to foreign economies. A billion-dollar increase in the trade deficit does not reflect a mere billion-dollar shift in economic activity; the net effect is many times greater. All sectors of the economy are hurt. Consumers benefit from lower-priced imports in the short run, but ultimately their source of income and purchasing power will be reduced by inevitable shifts in economic activity and economic growth in the exporting countries.

Sectoral Adjustment

The primary U.S. response to increased international competition in manufacturing has been a shift of resources to the service sector, which is essentially nontrade related. Growth in employment and capital investment has been felt in hotels, media properties, transportation, and retail sales. Price-earnings ratios in these sectors have risen sharply for existing companies, and new investment activity has increased rapidly. Such industries are attractive to investors because of their presumed immunity from foreign competition.

The performance of the service sector, however, is intimately linked to that of the industrial sector. A weak industrial sector reduces demand for services. Because most manufacturing industries are involved in trade, decreases in trade directly affect the well-being of the service industry. These decreases also adversely affect the public sector. Revenues decrease, while expenditure for social services increases. Debt rises, as do public borrowing and interest rates. In such situations, liberal monetary policies meant to stimulate the economy often make matters worse.

The U.S. economy has experienced the full negative effects of poor trade performance during the 1980s. The extended duration of this negative cycle, sustained by capital flows into the United States which have supported an overvalued dollar, has caused severe deterioration of the trade sector of the economy. Irreversible damage may have occurred in many segments of the U.S. economy, including agriculture. The textile industry, as the largest employer in the trade sector, provides, as we have tried to show, a clear case in point.

While the recent devaluation of the dollar against the yen and major European currencies may reduce pressure on the U.S. trade sector, it is unlikely to aid industries facing imports from Korea, Taiwan, and other NICs, whose currencies have not declined relative to the dollar. In addition, imports will continue to be supported by noncurrency factors such as low-cost capital, preferential tax treatment, subsidies, captive domestic markets, and other benefits provided to foreign firms by their governments. Currency adjustment of itself may not offset these factors.

A variety of public-policy initiatives might be used to strengthen the performance of the U.S. trade sector. Trade regulation and protectionism represent one set of options. U.S. trade policy has in fact become much more stringent in recent years. Bilateral agreements have limited textile imports, for example, but a series of trade restrictions have also been established in a range of industries. Recent trade rulings have imposed tariffs, duties, or quotas on products including lumber, steel, motorcycles, mobile phones and paging devices, optic fiber cable, and semiconductors. Trade negotiations have been initiated regarding market access for U.S. products in Korea, Japan, Brazil, the EEC, and elsewhere.

While protectionism has dramatically increased in popularity as a panacea for our trade woes, it offers little in the way of a long-term solution. In the short term, trade regulation can effectively offset the artificial effects of currency misalignment and foreign subsidies and can buffer cyclical volatility in trade activities. But as we have indicated, long-term protectionism reduces overall industrial efficiency, isolates industry from the forces of progress, and increases costs to consumers.

Recognition of the "locomotive" effect of the trade sector on the overall economy suggests that targeted stimulation of trade could lead to improvements felt throughout the economy. A $10 billion improvement in the balance of trade would result in tens of billions in increased economic activity, increased employment, reduction of public deficits, lower interest rates, and increased economic stability. During the Senate

Finance Committee's deliberations over the 1986 Tax Reform Bill, a measure was discussed which would have eliminated the Investment Tax Credit, except for investments in manufacturing, extraction, and communications facilities. This kind of selective investment incentive could stimulate investment in the trade sector, improve efficiency, quality, and responsiveness, and lead to better trade performance. Public incentives to encourage investment in automated, flexible manufacturing and information systems could also provide the genuine stimulus that the economy needs.

Enlightened public policy, therefore, combined with continued managerial innovation, could bring improved competitiveness to the textile industry and to the trade sector as a whole. There are signs that just these kinds of public and private initiatives are emerging at present. The question is timing. When the tide turns, how much of the U.S. industrial infrastructure will remain intact? How long will it take before the results of public-policy initiatives begin to appear in the nation's trade performance? Will U.S. industry be in a position to respond to a more favorable business environment? Even after decades of competition, the textile industry still is highly resilient. Although other industries may not fare as well, the present trade crisis requires a response.

Index

Page numbers in italics indicate figures; page numbers followed by t indicate tabular material.

About the Authors

Fariborz Ghadar is a professor and director of the International Business Program at the George Washington University School of Government and Business Administration. He is a specialist in international finance, global economic assessment, and the development of competitive corporate strategies. He has served as a consultant to a score of major corporations, governments, and government agencies. He was previously an investment officer at the World Bank/IFC in charge of English West African nations, as well as deputy minister in charge of export promotion and development with the government of Iran. His most recent publications include *The Multinational Enterprise in Transition* and *The Official Development Finance Programs of OECD Nations: A Comparative Study.* Professor Ghadar received a B.S. in chemical engineering and an M.S. in mechanical engineering from MIT and an M.B.A. and D.B.A. from Harvard Business School.

William H. Davidson is associate professor of management and organization at the University of Southern California. He has studied the issue of international competitiveness in several U.S. industries, and he is currently working on problems associated with managing international joint ventures and the management of technology. Professor Davidson is the author of *Revitalizing American Industry: The Lessons from our Competitors* and *The Amazing Race: Winning the Techno Rivalry with Japan.* He holds an A.B., M.A., and D.B.A. from Harvard University.

Charles S. Feigenoff is a well-known, Washington-based editorial consultant and writer for business and government. He is currently publications director and senior editor at the International Management Center. He has published numerous articles and books on international development and energy issues, most recently *The Official Develop-*

ment Finance Programs of OECD Nations: A Comparative Study. He is presently editing a forthcoming biography of Elliot White Springs, for many years the guiding force behind Springs Industries. Dr. Feigenoff earned his B.A. from Cornell University, his M.A. from the University of Colorado, and his Ph.D. from the University of Virginia.

A